The Twelve Degrees of Humility and Pride

The Twelve Degrees of Humility and Pride

by
Saint Bernard of Clairvaux

TAN Books
Gastonia, North Carolina

This edition of *The Twelve Degrees of Humility and Pride* was initially re-typeset from the edition published by The Macmillan Company, New York, 1929, and republished in 2013 by TAN Books as part of *The Foundations of Western Monasticism*. It was re-typeset and republished by TAN Books again in 2024.

Cover design by Caroline Green

ISBN: 978-1-5051-3395-0
Kindle ISBN: 978-1-5051-3397-4
ePUB ISBN: 978-1-5051-3396-7

Published in the United States by
TAN Books
PO Box 269
Gastonia, NC 28053

www.TANBooks.com

Printed in India

Table of Contents

Preface. vii
Author's Correction xxv
Author's Preface xxvii
Summary xxxi

PART ONE
The Twelve Degrees of Humility

Chapter One 3
Chapter Two 7
Chapter Three 11
Chapter Four 23
Chapter Five. 29
Chapter Six 33
Chapter Seven. 37
Chapter Eight 43
Chapter Nine 47

PART TWO

THE TWELVE DEGREES OF PRIDE

Chapter Ten 55

Chapter Eleven 71

Chapter Twelve 73

Chapter Thirteen 77

Chapter Fourteen 81

Chapter Fifteen 85

Chapter Sixteen 87

Chapter Seventeen. 89

Chapter Eighteen 91

Chapter Nineteen 95

Chapter Twenty 97

Chapter Twenty-One 99

Chapter Twenty-Two 101

Preface

Light in the Valley—From Law to Desire

By William Edmund Fahey, Ph.D.

The Roman mind of St. Benedict would have understood Leo XIII's re-organization (and rejuvenation) of the Benedictines in the nineteenth century. Finally recovering from the devastation of the Enlightenment and its Revolutions, the Catholic Church entered into a period of re-organization. Through the Papal brief *Summum Semper*, Leo brought together the scattered remnants of the Benedictine houses and—in an authoritative act—fashioned them into a single confederation or "order" under one Abbot Primate. Today, we bring to monasticism a largely nineteenth-century notion of a single, centralized order of Benedictine monks. Yet monasticism is again showing its diversity of forms and the Benedictines themselves have long been progressing back towards a decentralized model. There are currently twenty loosely affiliated congregations of Benedictines, seven of which date from after *Summer Semper*.

For all his *Romanitas*, St. Benedict did not intend a monolithic idea of an "order." His conception of monasticism was an attempt to understand how the Christian life could be lived purely and effectively. The confederation of monasteries that sprung out of his Rule was not a blueprint for a homogenized corporation. As the last chapter of the Rule makes clear, his directives were for beginners and envisioned modification and flexibility—much like the norms of classical Roman law and rule, in fact. By the tenth century, the various monastic communities in Western Europe had largely adopted the Rule of St. Benedict, while adapting it to local conditions and preserving, at least in part, ideas, customs, and rules taken from other authors. The Rule was successful in providing the essential architectural structure, but never envisioned uniformity, only unity of principles.

With its success came a diffusion of the vision and spirit of the Rule, as is often the case with organic and institutional growth: the further monasticism spread over geography and time, the less the fervor of the founding generation remained. Yet monastic literature and the Rule itself contained the principles of western monasticism's own reform, and its elasticity was limited, of course, by the Gospel and the life of grace. By the tenth century the spirit of development and renewal awoke in Europe, taking a northern and southern form.

In southern Europe, the desire for austerity was voiced anew by St. Romuald and St. Peter Damian. The anchoritic or hermitical fervor limited by St. Benedict rose up again to call Italian monasticism away from its distractions and, in some monasteries, its decadence. At the beginning of the eleventh century in the mountain valley of the Apennines near Arezzo, the Camoldoli movement began, harkening back to the most primitive roots of monasticism; and the solitude that was largely an interior solitude amongst Benedictines became once again a structural solitude. Men were not to be alone and apart for God while still amongst men, rather they were to be alone and apart physically. The Camodolese monks organized themselves over whole sections of mountain valleys in a form similar to eastern monasticism.

In northern Europe, the desire for austerity had resulted in a massive internal reform of Benedictines, first initiated by St. Benedict of Aniane (747–821), and then a century later by William Duke of Aquitaine's successful foundation of an abbey at Cluny in 910. The initial Cluniac reform was spurred on by a scholarly reawakening and a heightened sense of the world's fragility and the ultimate judgment of God.

Cluniac monasticism vigorously cultivated the private and corporate prayer life of its members. Corporate solitude was to be protected not only by the physical cloister, but by the aural cloister of near continual chant and vocal prayer. Under the dynamic direction of St. Hugh and with strong papal backing, Cluny, positioned in the very heart of France, became a vehicle for the far-reaching reinvention of monasticism and inspired two centuries of splendor in the liturgical arts and church architecture. In one of the most beautiful paradoxes in European history, a zeal for absolute concentration on the soul and a life of endless praise in the face of the end times led to one of the greatest bursts in material creativity and enrichment in Church history.

In response to the Cluniac development and the arguable departure from primitive Benedictine observance, a group of men originally associated with the monastery at Molesme, turned away for the marshy thickets of Cîteaux, twenty miles south of Dijon. On Palm Sunday in the year 1098, a monk named Robert (1028–1111) and a small group of disciples left their larger community to live as the early Christians, understanding the

Rule of St. Benedict as providing them a "formula of perfect penance" (*formula perfectae penitentiae*). A vision of this new life would soon be set out in the *Exordium Parvum*, one of the founding documents of a new kind of monastery. The members of the new association were to be poor men living with and contemplating a poor Christ, as they would say. Their common life, according to the Rule of St. Benedict, was to lead them back to a strict simplicity in all things exterior and interior. The perceived lavishness of the Cluniac-inspired Benedictines would be utterly rejected. Among the early founders was the English lawyer, St. Stephen Harding, whose hand was decisive in the *Exordium* and other early documents. These men were to be the Cistercians—the name originating from the simple place name for their new community: *Cistercium* in Latin (the site of modern Cîteaux), an abbreviation of *cis tertium* [*lapidem miliarum*] or "nearby the third milestone." How appropriate that men questing for simplicity would take their name from nothing more than a wayside road marker.

Behind this somewhat romantic narrative about the origins of this new branch of the Benedictine family was the common reforming spirit of the age. St. Robert of Molesme was seventy years-old in 1098. He had held a variety of positions within various monastic communities and clearly was restless in his pursuit of simplicity. At least three times prior to the attempt at Cîteaux, St. Robert had led groups of men into the wilds of France to establish hermitages. Molesme, which he would dramatically depart from and denounce, was initially his own attempt at a reformed Benedictine community. His early work had been fruitful; many were attracted to his austere zeal. St. Bruno, for example, who would eventually go on to found the most successful of the hermitical forms of western monasticism—the Carthusians—studied at Molesme under St. Robert in the 1070s. But ultimately St. Robert desired a more perfect form to structure his imitation and service of Christ. In his last attempt, he leaned heavily on St. Stephen Harding, a man marked by a deep understanding of the scholarship and legal reforms that were emerging throughout western Christendom.

For the new community at Cîteaux, law would take an almost mystical meaning. Law—the law of Benedict through his Rule and the laws or customs of the new Cistercian norms—was the means by which the Holy Spirit communicated His love. Obedience to the Rule of Benedict and the Cistercian documents led one to see the spiritual rectitude and purity that could be found in the selfless observations of rules in their integrity. Prayer life was simplified and the concept of pursuing an "ordered life," an *Ordo*, came to the fore. The "order" of Cistercian life re-emphasized things found in the Rule of St. Benedict—silence, mortification, manual labor—but recovered the centrality of charity as the objective. Observance of the law was not impersonal obedience, but the complete alignment of the monk's heart to the heart of Christ and to the will of the Father. In so doing, he would become a vessel of grace and love, untainted or diluted by the material riches or worldly apostolates (such as education, ornate liturgical craftsmanship, or diplomacy) that were increasingly becoming the expertise of the Cluniac Benedictines. It was into this setting, in the year 1113, under St. Stephen Harding as the third abbot of Cîteaux that a young Burgundian noble then named Bernard of Fontaines arrived with thirty companions, seeking Christ according to the principles of the new monastery.

The impossibility of adequately sketching the life St. Bernard of Clairvaux can be understood in Thomas Merton's remark that "Bernard contained the whole twelfth century in himself." Born for knighthood and adventure, St. Bernard (1090–1153) displayed his remarkable character most magnificently in his youthful rejection of either the straightforward pursuit of military and political prowess as a feudal lord or the apparently obvious route towards authority by way of the Cluniac monasticism. An inner impulse drove Bernard toward the austere vision of a kingly power which demanded displays of love and loyalty in the miry woods of Cîteaux. Yet in choosing the harder path of nascent Cistercian monasticism, Bernard would discover that all the functions of a feudal lord or powerful Churchman were not removed from his life, but only purified and multiplied under the laws of charity and the *ordo* of the Cistercian life which he would do much to shape and develop. St. Bernard would have a life filled with drama: interventions (political and ecclesial), public preaching, the reform of the papacy, the countering of grave theological and moral errors, and the organization of Christendom's greatest military endeavor—the Crusades—as well as its most best-known military order—the Templars. Finally, St. Bernard would oversee the reform or foundation of more than sixty monasteries; he stands as one of the most charismatic leaders in history.

The work which follows this introduction—*De Gradibus Superbiae et Humilitatis* (or *The Degrees of Humility and Pride*) was composed before Bernard of Fontaines was transformed by trial, conflict, and ardent fidelity into St. Bernard of Clairvaux, the "Doctor Mellifluus" of the Church. This was Bernard's first work. He had recently been sent by Stephen Harding along with a small group of followers to found a monastery in a marshy valley of Champagne, a site Bernard would name Clairvaux—"the clear valley"—testifying both to Bernard's humor and his faith-filled vision of what would rise up there. Despite a future punctuated by travel, he would remain the Abbot of Clairvaux until his death thirty seven years later. But 1115, the year of this work's appearance, witnessed little that could hint at future renown.

The life of the white-robed monks at Clarivaux was precarious, the health of their ascetic young abbot marked by illness, and the most basic material security of the establishment was a decade away. Those who know the restrained architecture that the Cistericians would later create or who envision something like that which inspired the "serene and blessed mood" which fell upon Wordsworth while walking near Tintern Abbey, must put aside such thoughts. The ideas fashioned to give monasticism its most mystical form were shaped under conditions on which men murmured for lack of food and the author spent many months in and out of the makeshift infirmary. Yet this is precisely what allowed the passionate heart of Bernard to develop the essential teaching of the Cistercians: that all the mortification and order of the monastic life was but preparation for the mercy and rapture of God's love.

For Bernard, men would ascend or descend, and they needed formal guidance on how to steady their souls, but the goal of monasticism was *an experience* of God's love beyond mere knowledge. The rules of Benedict were to keep the monk humble in their observation *and* in their breach, for God's intervening mercy would move the monk from the austere bruising of justice back towards the soul's ascent. Humility was the ladder to climb or fall, but even in falling, the ladder would remain for all who accepted the monastic life—not as a set of Pharisaical "rules," but as a path through one's own frailty and ever towards Christ. The Rule of Benedict was designed to strengthen the soul not only by successful ascent through the virtues, but through the hard yet necessary revelation of our vices. Only what was purified could be united to God. Bernard's early meditation marked a profoundly psychological turn into Catholic spirituality and the beginning of a sensual language that could strike some as distant from the spare *Romanitas* of St. Benedict. Yet these men are of a piece: without Benedict the lawgiver, Bernard the mystic would have no sturdy frame for his ardent contemplative journey. In the seventh chapter of Benedict's Rule, St. Bernard found the means for exploring the soul and working with God to return it to its Source, as a spouse gives her body to her true love. Readers of the *Ladder* should read and re-read that chapter as they move through this text.

Readers should note also the essential structure of the treatise: there are two basic parts, an exploration of the relationship between humility and truth, followed by a detailed analysis of the degrees or steps of pride and humility. The steps upon which Bernard focuses his attention are largely the precipitous steps taken in pride—steps that move one away from God—yet in honestly recognizing them for what they are, the Christian recognizes that an ascent can again begin in truth and through grace and mercy.

In the opening exposition on humility and truth, St. Bernard explains that our knowledge of the truth begins in humility and only with humility: we must understand ourselves as we really are. This perception of truth is then sharpened when we see others as ourselves—that is, as mortal men, limited and marred by sin and, like us, in need of mercy. The process by which we call for mercy on behalf of others and show mercy to others leads to the third stage of truth, the clear perception of what is true through contemplation of God. This contemplation is only possible because the heart has been utterly cleansed by grace, cleansed precisely because we have shown and, therefore, participated in God's mercy. While parts of this analysis can be found in both Christian and pagan authors, Bernard gives this exploration of the truth a Trinitarian dimension, pointing to the progressive aspect of mystical union. Christ the Son teaches us through our intellect first the purpose of humility. This stage is chiefly directed towards the self. The Holy Spirit enables man to love in charity, act with justice and show mercy through his will and actions. This stage is chiefly directed towards neighbors. God the Father leads the thoughtful and merciful man—like St. Paul—into the rapture of true Wisdom. The second half of the treatise carefully portrays the descending grades of the spiritual life with a delightful, humorous, and painfully accurate depiction of human self-deception and frailty.

This treatise, penned by the man whom the seventeenth-century Benedictine scholar Jean Mabillon called the "last of the fathers," displays the florid, patch-work style of the Patristic age, where a host of Church Fathers reinforce the principles of Scriptures and find themselves occasionally supported by unlikely pagan poets. The text is highly rhetorical. St. Bernard aims at the kind of delight alluded to in the words of the prophet Jeremiah: "Thou hast seduced me, Lord, and I let myself be seduced." (*Jer.*

20:7—*Seduxisti me, Domine, et seductus sum*). A principle of Cistercian spiritual writing from Bernard on is the movement of the person from carnal desire to spiritual desire. The language of love and desire and, indeed, the whole range of secular literature remain in place, but purified gently and progressively so that the soul does not cease to desire, but desires all the more its truest object: God.

Further Reading

The two best introductions to the early legislation and literature of the Cistercians may be found in:

The Cistercian World: Monastic Writings of the Twelfth Century, trans. and ed. P. Matarasso (London: Penguin Books, 1993). Contains selections from the found documents of Cîteaux, Bernard of Clairvaux, William of St. Thierry, Guerric of Igny, Aelfred of Rievaulx, and others.

The Great Beginning of Cîteaux: A Narrative of the Beginning of the Cistercian Order—The Exordium Magnum *of Conrad of Eberbach*, trans. Benedicta

Ward and P. Savage; ed. R. Elder (Kalamazoo, MI: Cistercian Publications, 2012).

General Studies

Stephen Tobin, *The Cistercians: Monks and Monasteries of Europe* (Woodstock and New York: The Overlook Press, 1995). Tobin's work is replete with excellent photographs and embeds the Cistercians in the social and political culture of medieval Europe.

J. B. Dalgairns, *Life of St. Stephen Harding, Abbot of Citeaux and Founder of the Cistercian Order*, ed. John Henry Newman, with notes by Herbert Thurston, S.J. (New York: Benzinger Brothers, 1898). Dalgairns was one of Newman's most committed students at Oxford and joined Newman in the founding of the English Oratorians. At Newman's suggestion he worked steadily with a company of scholars on the history of early English saints. This particular work provides important perspective for understanding the Cistercians and their significant English influence.

Louis Bouyer, *The Cistercian Heritage*, trans. E.A. Livingstone (Westminster, MD: The Newman

Press, 1958). The second and third chapters of this work focus on St. Bernard. Bouyer finally synthesizes the work of earlier generations with his own insights on Bernard. The book as a whole remains the best theological introduction to the Cistercian contribution.

L. J. Lekai, *The Cistercians: Ideal and Reality* (Kent, OH: Kent State University Press, 1977).

St. Bernard: his life and his impact on Catholic Spirituality

Cuthbert Butler, *Western Mysticism* (London: Constable, 1922).

G. R. Evans, *Bernard of Clairvaux* (Oxford: Oxford University Press, 2000).

Etienne Gilson, *The Mystical Theology of St. Bernard*, trans. A. H. C. Dowens (New York: Sheed and Ward, 1939). Gilson deftly applies a synthetic approach to St. Bernard's thought. On the one hand, the book is helpful for creating a structural unity to the varying creativity found in Bernard's writings. On the other hand, the coherence is at times more Gilson's than Bernard's—who like any prolific thinker develops his views from work to work and even within a single work, sometimes to an exasperating degree. Readers should not expect from St. Bernard himself the same kind of coherence that Gilson discloses.

Jean Leclercq, O.S.B., *Bernard of Clairvaux and the Cistercian Spirit*, trans. C. Lavoie (Kalamazoo, MI: Cistercian Publications, 1976). Dom Leclercq is perhaps the most thoughtful of Bernard's Benedictine students; his *Bernard of Clairvaux* is a delightfully written meditation.

Ailbe Luddy, *The Life and Teachings of St. Bernard* (Dublin: Gill, 1927).

Thomas Merton, O.S.C.O., *The Last of the Fathers: Saint Bernard of Clairvaux and the Encyclical Letter*, Doctor Mellifluus (New York: Harcourt Brace Jovanovich, 1954). Merton's own introduction carefully glosses and contextualizes the more visionary and general pronouncements of Pope Pius XII's encyclical.

Basil Pennington, O.C.S.O., "Introduction" in Bernard of Clairvaux, *The Steps of Humility and Pride*, trans. M. Ambrose Conway, O.C.S.O (Kalamazoo, MI: Cistercian Publications, 1989), pp. 1–24. This is the most careful analysis of Bernard's treatise in English.

John R. Sommerfeldt, The *Spiritual Teaching of Saint Bernard of Clairvaux* (Kalamazoo, MI: Cistercian Publications, 1991).

Author's Correction

In order to strengthen and support a certain opinion expressed in this little book I quoted the passage in the Gospel (*Mark* 13:32) in which Our Lord states that He was unaware of the date of the final Judgment. To this I inadvertently added a word which, as I have since discovered, does not occur in the Gospel. For the text has simply "*neither the Son knoweth,*" whereas I, thinking rather of the sense than of the wording, and with no intention to mislead, by mistake wrote: "*The Son of Man Himself knoweth not.*" (*Mark* 13:32) On this I based the whole of the subsequent argument, in which I attempted to prove the truth of my assertion by means of an inaccurate quotation. I did not discover my mistake until long after the publication of the pamphlet, and when a number of copies had been made. It is impossible to correct a mis-statement in a book which has had a wide circulation, so I have thought it incumbent on me to resort to the only possible remedy—an admission that I was wrong. And in another passage I have expressed a definite opinion about the Seraphim which I never heard, and have nowhere read. Here also my readers may well consider that it would have been more reasonable on my part to have said "I suppose," as I had certainly no desire to offer more than a conjecture on a matter which I was unable to prove from Scripture. It is also possible that the title chosen *Concerning the Degrees of Humility* may incur censure—but this will come only from those who overlook or misunderstand the meaning of that title—an explanation of which I have been careful to give in the conclusion of the tract.

—Saint Bernard

Author's Preface

You have asked me, brother Godfrey, to expand and put in writing the substance of the addresses *On the Degrees of Humility* which I had delivered to the brethren. I admit that, anxious as I was to give to this request of yours the serious answer that it deserved, I was doubtful whether I could comply with it. For with the evangelist's warning in my mind, I did not venture to begin the work, until I had sat down and calculated whether my resources were sufficient for its completion. Then, when love had cast out the fear that I had entertained of ridicule for failure to complete my work, it was replaced by misgiving of a different kind; for I was apprehensive of greater danger from the credit that might attend success than of the disgrace that might attach to failure. So I found myself, as it were, at the parting of the ways indicated respectively by affection and by fear; and I was long in doubt as to which was the safer choice. For I was afraid that if I said anything worth saying about humility, I might myself be found wanting in that virtue, whereas if, on grounds of modesty, I refused to speak, I might fail in usefulness. And I saw that, though neither of these courses is free from peril, I should be obliged to take one or the other. So I have thought it better to give you the benefit of anything that I can say, than to seek personal safety in the harbour of silence. And I earnestly trust that, if I am fortunate enough to say anything which commends itself to you, I may have in your prayers a safeguard against pride, whereas if—as is more likely—I produce nothing worthy of your attention, there will be no possible cause for conceit.

—Saint Bernard

DIAGRAM ILLUSTRATIVE OF "SCALA"

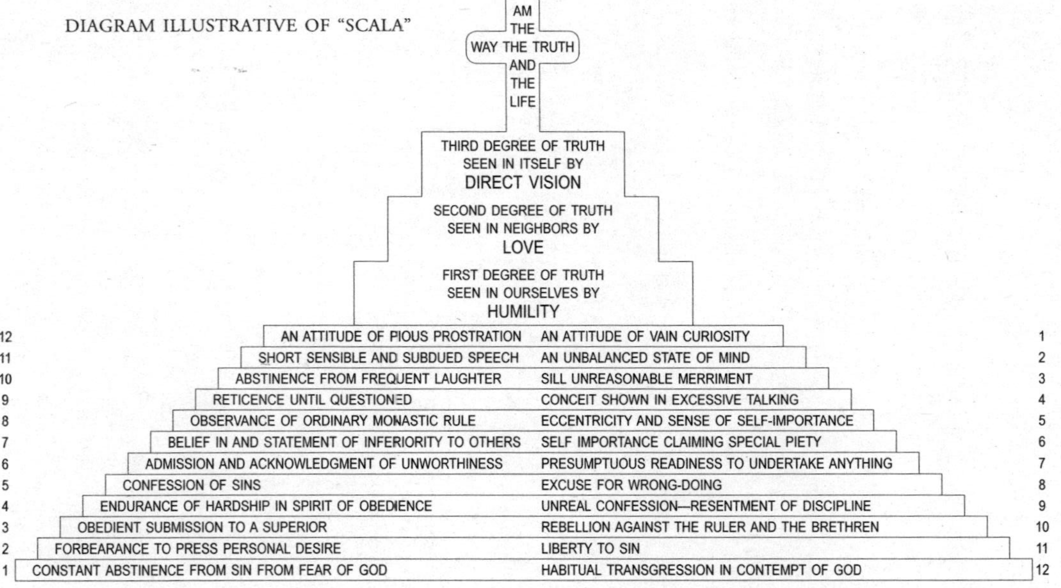

The first two stages of the ascent must be made before admission to the monastery.
The last two of the descent can be made only after departure or expulsion therefrom.

Summary

THE TWELVE DEGREES OF HUMILITY

The heads of the following book.[1]

1 These twelve degrees of humility are taken from the seventh chapter of the Rule of St. Benedict, the title of which is *Concerning Humility*. Its second paragraph runs thus: "Brethren, if we wish to arrive at the highest point of humility and speedily to reach that heavenly exaltation to which we can only ascend by the humility of this present life, we must by our ever-ascending actions erect such a ladder as that which Jacob beheld in his dream by which the Angels appeared to him descending and ascending. This descent and ascent signifieth nothing else than that we descend by self-exaltation and ascend by humility. And the ladder thus erected is our life in the world which if the heart be humbled, is lifted up by the Lord to heaven. The sides of the same ladder we understand to be our body and soul, in which our divine vocation hath placed various degrees of humility or discipline which we must ascend." (*Rule of St. Benedict*. Eng. Trans. by D. Oswald Hunter Blair, p. 43.)

This *scala* or "ladder" as constructed by St. Bernard, exhibits the plan and purpose of the treatise. The chart appended is an attempt to show how, in his opinion, the degrees of humility and of pride correspond to and counterbalance each other.

XII. A permanent attitude of bodily, and spiritual prostration.
XI. The speech of a monk should be short, sensible and in a subdued tone.
X. Abstinence from frequent and light laughter.
IX. Reticence, until asked for his opinion.
VIII. Observance of the general rule of the monastery.
VII. Belief in and declaration of one's inferiority to others.
VI. Admission and acknowledgment of one's own unworthiness and uselessness.
V. Confession of sins.
IV. Patient endurance of hardship and severity in a spirit of obedience.
III. Obedient submission to superiors.
II. Forbearance to press personal desire.
I. Constant abstinence from sin for fear of God.

These degrees of humility are set out in an ascending scale. The first two stages must be passed outside the monastic cloister. He who has so risen may thus in the third degree, make his submission to his superior.

THE TWELVE DEGREES OF PRIDE TAKEN DOWNWARDS

I. Curiosity, when a man allows his sight and other senses to stray after things which do not concern him.

II. An unbalanced state of mind, showing itself in talk unseasonably joyous and sad.

III. Silly merriment, exhibited in too frequent laughter.

IV. Conceit, expressed in much talking.

V. Eccentricity—attaching exaggerated importance to one's own conduct.

VI. Self-assertion—holding oneself to be more pious than others.

VII. Presumption—readiness to undertake anything.

VIII. Defence of wrong-doing.

IX. Unreal confession—detected when severe penance is imposed.

X. Rebellion against the rules and the brethren.

XI. Liberty to sin.

XII. Habitual transgression.

The two last named downward steps cannot be taken inside the cloister. The first six denote disregard for the brethren, the four following disrespect for authority, the two that remain contempt for God.

Part One

The Twelve Degrees of Humility

Chapter One

The search for Truth—Christ the goal and the road

I propose to speak of the degrees of humility, as St. Benedict sets them before us, as not only to be enumerated but to be attained. And I will first indicate, to the best of my ability, the goal that may be reached by their means, so that when you have heard the result of its attainment, the toil involved in the ascent may be less severely felt. So let our Lord set before us the difficulties that we shall encounter, and the reward that we shall receive for our toilsome journey.

I *am*, saith He, *The Way and the Truth and the Life*. (*John* 14:6). He calls humility "the way" because it leads to the truth. In the former lies the labour, in the latter is the reward. But, you may ask, how am I to know that He was here speaking of humility, since He says without further explanation, *I am the Way*? Listen to His more explicit statement, *Learn of me because I am meek and humble of heart.* (*Matt.* 11:29). In this He exhibits Himself as a type of humility, a model of meekness. If you imitate Him, you are not walking in darkness, but you will have the light of life. What is the light of life, unless it be the truth, which lightens every man that comes into the world, and shows us wherein true life consists? For this reason, to those words of His *I am the Way and the Truth*, He added *and the Life*, as though He meant to say, I am the way because I lead to the truth, I am the truth because I promise life, I am myself the life which I give. *For this*, saith He, *is life eternal, that they may know thee the true God, and Jesus Christ whom thou hast sent.* (*John* 17:3). But admitting this, you may still say, I recognize humility as the way; I long for truth as the reward; but what if the toil of the journey be so great that I am unable to reach the desired goal? To this He replies, *I am the life*, that is the provision for the journey by which you will be supported on the way. So He exclaims to the wanderers and to those who do not know the road, *I am the way*, to the doubters and disbelievers, *I am the truth*, to those who have begun the ascent and are getting tired, *I am the life*.

I think that it has been made sufficiently clear by the passage quoted from the Gospel that the reward of humility is the apprehension of the truth. And take another passage, *I praise thee, Father of heaven and earth, because thou hast hidden these things* (that undoubtedly means "secret truths") *from the wise and prudent* (that is from the proud) *and hast revealed them unto babes* (that is to the humble). (*Matt.* 11:25).

This affords further evidence that the truth which is withheld from the proud, is disclosed to the humble. And the following may be taken as the definition of humility. It is the virtue which enables a man to see himself in his true colours and thereby to discover his worthlessness. And this is the characteristic virtue of those *who are disposed in their hearts to ascend by steps* from virtue to virtue, until they reach the summit of humility; where, standing on Sion as on a watch-tower, they may survey the truth. For, saith the Psalmist, *the law-giver shall give a blessing*. He then who gave the law will also provide the blessing—that is to say, he who has prescribed humility will conduct us to the truth. And who is this lawgiver but the kind and righteous Lord who has given a law to those who fail in the way? And surely those who have forsaken the truth have failed on the way. But are they on that account forsaken by the kind Lord? Nay, but it is for these very persons that the kind and righteous Lord prescribes the path of humility, by their return to which they may discover the truth. He allows them an opportunity of regaining salvation because He is kind, yet not without the discipline of law because He is righteous. In His kindness He will not permit their ruin, in His righteousness He cannot omit their punishment.

Chapter Two

The ladder of humility, foreshadowed by that which Jacob saw in his vision. The refreshment provided by Christ—humility, love, and contemplation—of which love is the central course, as on Solomon's table.

St. Benedict enumerates twelve degrees in this law by which the return to truth is made; so that as access to Christ is gained when the Ten Commandments and the two-fold circumcision—which together make up the number of twelve—have been passed, truth may likewise be attained by passing through these twelve degrees. And what can be the significance of the fact that the Lord appeared leaning over that ladder which was shown to Jacob as a symbol of humility, but that the recognition of truth begins when the height of humility is reached? For then the Lord, whose eyes, as He is the embodiment of truth, could neither deceive nor be deceived, was looking down from the top of that ladder over the sons of men—to discover whether there is anyone who understands or seeks after God. And does He not seem to you to cry aloud from on high and to say to those who seek Him (for He knows who are His) *Come over to me ye who desire me, and be filled with fruits* (*Ecclus.* 24:26), and also, *Come unto me ye who labour and are burdened and I will refresh you*? (*Matt.* 11:28). But what refreshments is this that Truth promises to those who attempt and gives to those who attain? Is it perchance love? Then this it is at which, as St. Benedict says, the monk who has passed through all the degrees of humility will ere long arrive. Truly love is delightful and pleasant food, supplying, as it does, rest to the weary, strength to the weak, and joy to the sorrowful. It in fact renders the yoke of truth easy and its burden light.

Love is good food, which, as the central dish on Solomon's dinner table, by the aroma of various virtues as by the fragrance of different condiments, refreshes those who are hungry and delights those who give the refreshment. For on it are set out peace, patience, kindness, forbearance, *joy in the Holy Ghost* (*Rom.* 14:17); and if there are any other products of truth or of wisdom, they too are there. Humility also has her dishes on the same tray, namely, the bread of affliction and the wine of remorse. These are the things which Truth offers in the first place to beginners, for to them it is said, *Rise after ye have sat down, ye who eat the bread of sorrow.* There also contemplation has its solid food, made of the fat essence of the corn, and the wine that maketh glad the heart of man. To this food Truth invites those who have accomplished their course, saying: *Eat, my friends, and drink and be inebriated, my dearly-beloved. The midst,* saith he, *he covered with love, for the daughters of Jerusalem* (*Cant* 3:10)—that is to say, for the sake of the immature souls which, while they are as yet unable to receive solid food, must meanwhile be fed with the milk of love instead of with bread, and with oil instead of with wine. And love is rightly called the central course, because beginners are unable, through their timidity, to take advantage of its sweetness, while to those who have arrived at maturity it is an insufficient substitute for the deeper delight of full vision. The first still require to be cleansed, by a very bitter dose of fear, from the pestilent poison of fleshly lust, and have not yet discovered the sweetness of milk. The latter have already turned away from milk and are revelling in the delight derived from their entrance into glory. Those only in the middle—who are on the journey—have found some delicious little morsels of love, with which, owing to their weak digestion, they so far have to be content.

So the first course is humility, purifying by its bitterness, the second is love, comforting by its sweetness, the third is full vision, secure in its strength. *Alas for me, Lord God of righteousness—how long wilt thou be angry against the prayer of thy servant, how long wilt thou feed me with the bread of tears and give me tears for my drink?* (*Ps.* 70:5; 69:5, Vulg.). Who will call me even so far as to that delightful company of love, where the righteous feast in the sight of God, and revel in the fulness of their joy; where I need no longer speak in the bitterness of my heart, but may say to God "condemn me not," if while I feast on the unleavened bread of sincerity and of truth, I sing joyously in the paths of the Lord, for great is the glory of the Lord? Yet good also is the path of humility, for by it truth is sought, love is reached, and a share of the fruits of wisdom is obtained. As in a way Christ is the end of the law, so is He the perfection of humility, and the final apprehension of truth. Christ when He came brought grace. Truth gives grace to those to whom it has become known. But as it is by the humble that it is known, it is to them that it gives grace.

Chapter Three

The process by which the road of humility leads to the attainment of Truth. The three degrees of Truth. The teaching of Christ about these. Discussion of the difficulty involved in the statement that He learned compassion through suffering.

I have stated, as well as I can do so, the blessings to be gained by passing upwards through the degrees of humility. I will now, to the best of my ability, explain the process by which these lead to the promised prize—the attainment of truth. But as the recognition of truth is gradual, I will, if I can do so, indicate its three degrees, in order to make it more clear to which of these the twelfth degree of humility leads.

We seek for truth in ourselves, in our neighbours, and in its essential nature. We find it first in ourselves by severe self scrutiny, then in our neighbours by compassionate indulgence, and, finally, in its essential nature by that direct vision which belongs to the pure in heart. Observe both the number and the sequence. To begin with, let Him who is the Truth teach you that you must search for truth in those around you before you look for it in its intrinsic purity. You will afterwards learn why you must search for it in yourself before you do so in your neighbours. Thus in the enumeration of the Beatitudes in His Sermon He placed "the merciful" before "the pure in heart." For the merciful quickly discover truth in their neighbours when they extend their sympathy to them, and so kindly identify themselves with them that they feel their good and evil characteristics as if they were their own. They are weak with those that are weak, with those who are offended they burn. They have made it their habit to *rejoice* with *them that rejoice and weep with them that weep.* (*Rom.* 12:15). When their spiritual vision has been made clear and acute by this brotherly love, they delight to gaze on truth for its own sake, and in their affection for it they are indulgent towards errors which are not their own. But how can those who, so far from thus associating themselves with their brethren, insult them in their sorrow and deride them in their joy, possibly discern truth in their neighbours, seeing that they cannot enter into the feelings of others about things of which they have no personal experience? Well, indeed, does the common saying fit them "a healthy man has no idea of the feelings of one who is ill, nor does a well-fed man realize what a hungry man suffers." A sick man feels for the sick and a hungry man for the hungry, with familiarity the greater as his own condition approaches theirs. For as pure truth can be discerned only by one whose heart is pure, so can the sorrow of a brother be most truly felt by one whose heart is sad. But if your heart is to be saddened by the sorrows of others, you must recognize your own evil state, which you may see reproduced in your neighbour, and may thus know how to help him. And in this you have the example of our Saviour, who was willing to suffer that He might know how to sympathize, to accept sorrow that He might thus learn to pity. For, as it is written of Him, *He learned obedience by the Things which He suffered*, so may He have suffered that He might learn compassion. This, however, does not mean that He, whose compassion was eternal in its origin and its duration, had not hitherto known pity, but that what He knew in His nature in an eternal, He learned by experience in a temporal, sphere.

But you may find it difficult to accept my statement that Christ who is the Divine wisdom "learned compassion," as though it were possible for Him through whom all things were made, ever to have been ignorant of anything; especially in view of the fact that the passage from the Epistle to the Hebrews which I have adduced in support of my argument, may be understood in a different sense, which would not involve us in this difficulty. For, on this interpretation, the words "*He learned*" would refer, not to His own Person, but to His body which is the Church. In that case the meaning of the sentence, *And He learned obedience by the things that He suffered* would *be that He learned obedience* in His body through what He personally suffered. For what was the meaning of that death, that cross, those insults, spittings and stripes, all of which Christ who is our head endured, unless that they afford to us who are His body, convincing evidence of His Obedience? *For Christ*, saith Paul, became *obedient to his Father, even unto death.* (*Phil* 2:8). And what was the need for such obedience? Let the Apostle Peter give the answer: *Christ suffered for us leaving to you an example that you should follow his steps* (*1 Pet.* 2:21), that is that you shall imitate His obedience. So from His sufferings we learn how much we, who are mere men, must be prepared to endure for the sake of obedience, in the exercise of which He, who is also God, did not hesitate to die. And this, you may say, is the sense in which it is not unreasonable to allege that Christ learned obedience or compassion, or anything else during His earthly life, although you at the same time believe that it was not possible for Him to acquire while on earth any knowledge which He did not previously possess in His divine Person. Thus He might Himself both learn and teach pity and obedience, since the head and the body is one Christ.

I do not deny that this verse may reasonably be thus understood. But the former interpretation seems to be supported by another passage in the same Epistle, in which it is said *For nowhere doth he take hold of the angels, but of the seed of Abraham he taketh hold, wherefore it behoved him in all things to be like unto his brethren, that he might become merciful.* (*Heb.* 2:16). I think that these words have so close a reference to His Person, that they cannot be altogether applicable to His body. It is at any rate said of the word of God that He "took," that is He incorporated into His own personality, not "angels" but "the seed of Abraham." For the passage reads not "the word was made an angel" but *the Word was made flesh* (*John* 1:14), and that from the flesh of Abraham, in accordance with the promise made to him. *Whereupon*, that is by reason of this assumption of the seed, *he ought in all things to be like unto his brethren*, that is to say, it was right and necessary that He should be, as we are, susceptible to suffering and should share with us every kind of misfortune with the exception of sin. If you ask "Wherefore this necessity?" the answer is *that*

He may become merciful. And, you may say, why may not this be properly understood as referring to His body? But listen to the words which so closely follow these. *For in that wherein he himself hath suffered and been tempted; he is able to succour them also that are tempted.* (*Heb*. 2:18). And for these words I can see no better meaning than that He was pleased thus to suffer and to be tempted and to associate Himself with all human misery except sin—which is what being "like unto his brethren in all things" means, in order that He might learn by personal experience to pity and to feel for those who similarly suffer and are tempted. I do not say that this experience added to His knowledge, but that it brought Him closer to us, so that the weak sons of Adam whom He has not disdained to make His own and to call His brethren, need not hesitate to bring their infirmities to Him, who, recognizing what He has Himself endured, as God is able and as their neighbour is desirous to provide the remedy. For this reason Isaiah calls Him a man *of sorrows and acquainted with infirmity* (*Is*. 43:3), and the Apostle says, *We have not a High Priest who cannot have compassion on our infirmities.* (*Heb*. 4:15). And to show how He can have such compassion the writer adds, *but one tempted in all things like as we are, without sin.* For surely the blessed God, while in that form in which He thought it not robbery to be equal with God, was beyond doubt incapable of suffering before He had emptied Himself; and taken the form of a slave; and as He had no experience of sorrow or of subjection, He had no opportunity of practicing either compassion or obedience. He had indeed a natural but not an experimental knowledge of these. Yet as He not only laid aside His own dignity, but was made a little lower than the angels, who by favour not by nature are incapable of suffering, He took a form in which it was possible for Him to suffer and to submit, which, as has been stated, He could not have done in that form which was His own. Thus by suffering He learned compassion and by subjection obedience. This experience, however, led, as I have pointed out, to an increase, not of Wisdom on His part, but of confidence on ours, since by the knowledge thus painfully acquired He from whom we had been so widely separated was brought nearer to us. For when would we dare to approach Him while He was incapable of suffering? But now the Apostle advises and exhorts us *to go with confidence to the throne of grace* (*Heb*. 4:16) whereon is He whom we surely recognize as the one of whom it is elsewhere written that *He hath borne our infirmities and carried our sorrows* (*Is*. 43:4), and of whose power to sympathize with us in what He has himself endured we can entertain no doubt.

So there appears to be no contradiction on the one hand, in saying that, as there is nothing of which Christ was ever unaware, His knowledge could have no commencement, and, on the other hand, in maintaining that while in His Divine nature, He knew compassion from all eternity; in another capacity He learned it under bodily and temporal conditions. And note the similar language which our Lord used when in reply to a question from His disciples. He pleaded ignorance of the date of the Last Day. For how could He in whom *are hid all the treasures of wisdom and knowledge* (*Col.* 2:3) be unaware of that day? How could He, for whom ignorance of any sort was clearly impossible, say that He did not know? Could He possibly desire to conceal by a subterfuge, information which He could not profitably disclose? God forbid the thought! For neither could He who is Wisdom be unaware of anything, nor could He who is Truth be capable of falsehood. But in His desire to discourage the useless curiosity of the disciples, He pleaded ignorance of the matter about which they asked Him—not indeed without qualification but in a way in which He could truth-fully disclaim such knowledge. For although by His Divine insight—ranging over all things past, present and future, He had that day clearly before Him, it was still true that He was unaware of it by the exercise of any bodily sense. Had it been otherwise He would already have slain Antichrist with the breath of His mouth, would have heard with His bodily ears the shout of the archangel and the sound of the trumpet at whose call the dead are to rise, and would have surveyed with His bodily eyes the sheep and the goats who are then to be separated from each other.

But with the intention of making it clear that it was only in the sphere of that intelligence which He possessed in His human capacity that he asserted His ignorance of that day, He was careful in His answer not to say "I do not know" but "The Son of Man himself doth not know." Now what is this title of "Son of Man" but the one which He assumed on taking on Himself our nature? By its use here, He means it to be understood that when He says that He is ignorant of anything, He is speaking not as God, but as man. When on the other hand He refers to His own Godhead, He usually says not "the Son" or "the Son of Man" but "I" or "We"—as in the passage *verily verily I say unto you, before Abraham was made, I am.* (*John* 8:58). He there speaks of Himself as "I" not as the "Son of Man." There can be no doubt that He then referred to that existence which was His before Abraham, and which never had a beginning—not to what He became after the time of Abraham and by descent from him. And when

He elsewhere asks His disciples what men think of Him, He says *Whom do men say* not "that I am" but that *the Son of Man is?* (*Matt.* 16:13, 16). But when He afterwards asks the same disciples what they themselves felt about Him, He says, *But whom do you say* not "that the Son of Man is," but *that I am?* So when He asks the opinion of worldly persons about His bodily nature He uses the term "Son of Man," but when He questions His spiritual followers about His Godhead, He significantly says not "the Son of Man" but "me." And that Peter understood what He meant by putting the question in this form is apparent from his reply, for he says *Thou art*, not "Jesus the son of a Virgin," but *Christ the Son of God.* Had he made the former reply he would have said what is no less true. But shrewdly gathering from the wording of the question the meaning of Him who put it, he gave a suitable and sufficient answer by saying, *Thou art Christ the Son of God.*

Now from this you may see that Christ has two natures, albeit in one Person, one in which He has always existed, the other in which He had a beginning, and that while in that nature which is eternal He always knew everything, in that which is temporal He found out many things in the course of time. Why then do you find it difficult to admit that as there was a time when His bodily existence began, so may His knowledge of the ills of the flesh—at all events that sort of knowledge which bodily weakness conveys—have had a beginning? Our first parents would no doubt have been better and wiser had they not possessed knowledge of this sort, since they could acquire it only through folly and misfortune. But God, their Creator, seeking what had been lost, in His mercy followed up His own handiwork. He Himself mercifully descended to the level from which they had miserably fallen, and was willing Himself to endure what they deservedly suffered through their disobedience to Him—and this not from a curiosity like theirs, but from marvelous love, His purpose being not to remain in misery with the unfortunate, but to become merciful and so to deliver them from their misery. When I say that he became merciful I refer not to that compassion which had been His in His eternal condition of bliss, but to that which He acquired through the medium of misfortune, while He bore our nature. Moreover, He completed in the latter the work of love which He had commenced in the former state. He could undoubtedly have made it complete in the former alone, but without the latter it would not have been effectual for us. Both forms were essential, but the latter more closely concerns ourselves. How indescribable is the method of His goodness. Could we ever have understood that marvellous mercy unless previous suffering had given it shape? Could we have discerned His sympathy, of which we had no knowledge, if He had had no previous suffering and had remained insusceptible to pain? Yet had He not possessed that compassion which knows no misfortune, He would never have attained that whose mother is misfortune. If He had not attained this He could not have drawn it to Himself. If He had not so drawn it, He could not have brought it out. And whence did He bring it out if not *from the pit of misery and mire of dregs?* (*Ps.* 40:2; 39:3, Vulg.). Yet He did not abandon that earlier compassion, but added to it the later. He did not alter, He augmented it, as it is written, *Men and beasts thou wilt preserve, O God, O how hast thou multiplied thy mercy, O God.* (*Ps.* 36:6, 7; 35:7, 8, Vulg.).

Chapter Four

*The first degree of Truth—self-scrutiny—
reveals to us our own evil case.*

But let us resume the thread of our argument. If then He in whose nature there was no sadness, made Himself sad in order that He might have personal experience of something of the existence of which He was already aware, how much more is it your duty, I will not say to alter, but to recognize your condition, which is indeed a pitiable one—and thus to learn compassion of which you could otherwise have no knowledge? For it may well happen that by dwelling on the shortcomings of your neighbour without sufficient attention to your own, you may be moved not to pity but to anger—not to assist but to condemn, and so to destroy in a spirit of wrath, rather than to restore in a spirit of meekness. Ye who are spiritual, saith the Apostle, instruct such an one in the spirit of meekness. The counsel—aye, the command—of the Apostle is that you should aid your ailing brother in the same kindly spirit in which you would wish to be helped when you are ailing. And to show how it is possible to be forbearing towards a wrong-doer, he says, considering thyself lest thou also be tempted. And please to note how well the disciple of Truth follows the sequence of the Master. In the Beatitudes, to which I have already referred, the "merciful" are named before the "pure in heart," as are the "meek" before the "merciful." And the Apostle when he exhorted those who were spiritual to restore such as were carnal, added in the spirit of meekness. For the reformation of the brethren is the mark of the merciful, and a spirit of meekness that of the humble. He says in effect that no one who is not himself meek can be reckoned among the merciful. Note that the Apostle here clearly asserts exactly what I said just now that I would establish, viz., that truth must be sought in ourselves before we can look for it in others, for he says consider thyself—by which he means, think how easily you may be tempted—how liable you are to sin—so that by self-scrutiny you may be made humble and may thus come to the aid of others in a spirit of meekness. If, however, you heed not the warning of the Apostle, tremble before the rebuke of the Master. Thou hypocrite, cast out first the beam out of thine own eye and thus shalt thou see to cast out the mote out of thy brother's eye. (Matt. 7:5). Pride in the mind is like a thick heavy beam in the eye, whose excessive size is due not to health but to vanity, to swelling rather than to strength. It so darkens the mental vision as to hide the truth. If then it has taken hold of your mind, you will be unable to see yourself as you really are, or to appreciate either your actual or possible condition, but you will fancy that you are or will become just what you would like to be. For what is pride if not—as a certain holy man defines it "appreciation of one's own goodness." If this be so, we may say, on the other hand, that humility is the disparagement of our own goodness. For love and hatred alike ignore the verdict of truth. Would you like to hear what that verdict is? As I hear so I judge (John 5:30), not as "I hate" or "I love" nor as "I fear." There is the judgment of hate, such as that which said We have a law and according to our law he ought to die. (John 19:7). And there is the judgment of fear like that one If we let him alone so the Romans will come and take away our place and nation. (John 11:48). But there is a judgment of love, as that of David on the son who would have slain his father, Spare the boy Absalom. And I know that it is a rule of human law, which is binding alike in ecclesiastical and in civil actions, that personal friends of the litigants shall not be allowed to take part in the proceedings lest through their affection for their friends they may be misled or may mislead others. And if affection for a friend leads you to extenuate or even to conceal his guilt, how much more will self-esteem preclude an unfavourable verdict upon yourself? So the man who is really anxious to discover the truth about himself must remove the beam of pride which prevents him from seeing the light, and must propose in his heart to ascend by steps by which he may scrutinize his inmost self, and from the twelfth degree of humility may pass on to the first degree of truth. But when a man has found truth in himself—or rather has found himself in truth—so that he can say, I have believed and therefore have I spoken, but I have been humbled exceedingly, he may rise to a high spiritual level in order that truth may be held up, and may say in his ecstasy, Every man is a liar. Do you not suppose that this was the trend of David's thought? Do not you think that the prophet felt as did the Lord, as did the Apostles, and as we do who come after them and share their feelings? I believed, says this man, in Truth who says, He that followeth me walketh not in darkness. (John 8:12). I therefore showed my faith by following, and expressed it by confessing. And by confessing what? The truth—which I discovered through faith. But afterwards I believed unto righteousness and made confession unto salvation. I was humbled exceedingly (Ps. 116:10; 115:10, Vulg.), that is entirely. He appears to mean by this—since I was not ashamed of the fact that the truth which I discerned in myself bore witness against me, I carried humility to its utmost extent. For this word "exceedingly" may mean "completely," as in the passage, He shall delight exceedingly in his commandments. (Ps. 112:1; 111:1, Vulg.). But someone may urge that "exceedingly" is here used for "in a high degree," not for "completely" and that the commentators seem to uphold this interpretation. Even if this be so, there is nothing inconsistent with the meaning of the Prophet, which we may take as being to this effect:

> While I was still unaware of the truth, I did indeed suppose myself to be something—whereas I was nothing. But when I afterwards believed in Christ and therefore tried to imitate His humility, I recognized the truth. It was indeed uplifted in me by my confession, but I was *exceedingly humbled*, that is, was greatly depreciated in my own estimation as a result of my self-scrutiny.

Chapter Five

The second degree of Truth—wherein consciousness of our own shortcomings makes us merciful to those of other people.

Thus in this, the first degree of Truth, the Prophet is so humbled that he says in another Psalm, *In thy truth thou hast humbled me.*(*Ps.* 119:75; 118:75, Vulg.). He may then reasonably conclude that the wretched condition in which he finds himself to be, is that of mankind in general. And as he thus passes into the second degree, he may say in his ecstasy, *Every man is a liar.* (*Ps.* 116:11; 115:11 Vulg.). And in what does this ecstasy consist? Is it not without doubt due to the fact that in his detachment from himself and attachment to truth, he pronounced his own condemnation? So in that ecstatic condition he may say, not in anger or insult—but with pity and regret, *Every man is a liar.* And why is every man a liar? Every man is weak, every man is poor and powerless, since none can save himself or anyone else. In much the same sense is it said, *Vain is the horse for safety* (*Ps.* 33:17; 32:17 Vulg.), not because the horse deceives anyone but because the rider deceives himself if he relies on the horse's strength. So every man is said to be false, that is, fragile and fickle, because no one can hold out any assurance of safety to himself or to others, and anyone who puts his trust in man is more likely to receive condemnation. Thus the humble Prophet, proceeding under the guidance of Truth, observes in other people what he mourns in himself; where he finds knowledge he will also find sorrow, and so may say broadly but truly, *Every man is a liar.* Now note how widely different was the tone of that haughty Pharisee. What was the purport of his ill-considered utterance? *God, I give thee thanks that I am not as the rest of men.* (*Luke* 18:11). While he is strangely satisfied with himself, he is offensively rude to others. David takes quite another line. He says *Every man is a liar.* He will make no exceptions which might be misleading, for he knows that *all have sinned and all do need the glory of God.* (*Rom.* 3:23). The Pharisee, while condemning others claims exemption for himself alone. The Prophet does not exempt himself from the general guilt, lest he be excluded from mercy. The Pharisee stifles mercy by his disclaimer of guilt. The Prophet asserts, of himself as of every one, *Every man is false.* The Pharisee endorses this of all except himself, when he says, *I am not as the rest of men.* And he returns thanks not that he is good, but that he stands alone—not so much for his own merits as for the ill which he sees in others. He has not yet cast out the beam out of his own eye, but he reckons up the motes in the eyes of his brethren—for he adds, *unjust, extortioners.* I think that this diversion from the subject may not have been without its value, if it has enabled you to appreciate the difference between these two utterances.

Let us now return to the main subject. If truth thus compels men to look into themselves and so to learn their own worthlessness, it follows as an inevitable consequence that all those things which have hitherto given them pleasure—yea, even their own selves—should become distasteful to them. For as they sit in judgment upon themselves, they cannot fail to see themselves in a light in which they are ashamed to be seen even by their own eyes. Their present condition displeases them and they long to be what they are not—a result which they distrust their power to achieve. Yet they find their consolation in the fact that their judgment of themselves has been stern and severe; and they hope that their love of truth and their hunger and thirst after righteousness—even to the point of self-contempt—will enable them to exact a strict satisfaction for the past and to effect a real amendment in the future. But when they perceive their incapacity for any adequate and extensive reform, and realize that when they have done all that is commanded they must still call themselves unprofitable servants, they fly from justice to mercy. And that they may obtain this they follow the advice given by Truth, *Blessed are the merciful, for they shall obtain mercy.* (*Matt.* 5:7). This then is the second degree of truth, the one in which men look for it in their neighbours—when from the realization of their own shortcomings they discover those of other people and learn from their own painful experience to sympathize with those who suffer.

Chapter Six

The third degree of Truth—the clearing of the spiritual sight, so that it may gaze on holy and heavenly things.

If therefore men practice perseverance in the three matters that have been mentioned—*viz.*, the sorrow of repentance, the longing for righteousness, and works of mercy, they clear their spiritual sight of the three hindrances which either through ignorance, infirmity or disposition they have encountered, and may thus pass on to that direct vision in which the third degree of truth consists. These are the ways that seem good to men—at all events to those *who are glad when they have done evil and rejoice in most wicked things*, and who attempt to cover their sins with the cloak of ignorance or of weakness. But vainly do they whose ignorance or weakness is wilful put forward either of these pleas as an excuse for indulgence in sin. Do you suppose that the first man could successfully plead infirmity of the flesh on the ground that he sinned, not of his own accord, but at the instigation of his wife? Or were the men who stoned the first martyr, and had themselves stopped their ears, excusable on the plea of ignorance? Some people think that they have a natural antipathy to truth, and an inclination to and affection for sin, and that they are overcome by weakness and ignorance. Let such persons turn inclination into aversion, affection into distaste; let them conquer the weakness of the flesh by righteous energy, and dispel ignorance by better education. For if they disregard truth now, when it is needy, naked and weak, they may recognize it to their shame too late, when, coming with full authority and power, it overawes and rebukes them. They will then tremble as they return the vain reply, *When did we see thee in need, and did not minister to thee?* Surely the Lord whom they now disregard when He seeks sympathy *shall be known when he executeth judgments.* (*Ps.* 9:16; 9:17, Vulg.). Finally *they look on him whom they pierced* (*John* 19:37)—as shall also the covetous on him whom they despised. Thus by the tears of penitence, by the pursuit of righteousness and by persistence in works of mercy, is the spiritual sight cleared from all stain, whether due to weakness, ignorance or disposition. And to it truth promises to reveal itself in its purity. *Blessed are the clean of heart, for they shall see God.* (*Matt.* 5:8).

There are then three kinds of degrees of truth; we rise to the first by humble effort, to the second by loving sympathy, to the third by enraptured vision. In the first truth is revealed in severity, in the second in pity, in the third in purity. Reason, by which we analyze ourselves, guides us to the first, feeling which enables us to pity others conducts us to the second; purity by which we are raised to the level of the unseen, carries us up to the third.

Chapter Seven

The work of the Persons of the Holy Trinity in leading men through the three degrees of Truth.

Here I seem to discern a certain marvelous and individual operation of each Person of the Trinity—if indeed it is possible for the limited intelligence of man to conceive a difference such as cannot be expressed in words between persons who co-operate. On this supposition, the first degree appears to be due to the action of the Son, the second to that of the Holy Spirit, and the third to that of the Father. Would you wish to hear about the work of the Son? *If*, saith He, *I, your Lord and Master, have washed your feet, how much more ought ye to wash one another's feet.* The Master of truth thus presented to His disciples a pattern of humility, that they might therein discern the first degree of truth. Mark also the work of the Holy Spirit, *Love is poured forth in our hearts by the*

Holy Ghost which is given to us. (*Rom.* 5:8). Love is indeed the gift of the Holy Spirit, and this makes it possible for those who, under the instruction of the Son, have by humility already attained the first degree of truth, under the guidance of the Holy Spirit to reach the second by sympathy with their neighbours. Hear also what is said about the Father. *Blessed art thou Simon Bar Jona, because flesh and blood hath not revealed it to thee, but my father who is in heaven.* (*Matt.* 16:17). And there is another passage, *The father shall make thy truth known to the children.* (*Is.* 38:19). And yet again, *I thank thee, Father, because thou hast hid these things from the wise and hast revealed them to little ones.* (*Matt.* 30:25). You see then how the Father at last receives into glory those to whom the Son first taught humility by precept and by practice, and on whom the Holy Spirit then shed love. The Son receives them as learners, the Comforter encourages them as friends, the Father raises them as sons. For this reason the title of "The truth" is rightly given, not only to the Son, but also to the Father and to the Holy Ghost. From this it follows that one and the same truth—preserving the characteristics of each of the Persons—performs this threefold work in the three degrees. In the first one it gives instruction as does a master; in the second it affords counsel as does a friend or a brother; in the third it provides a bond of union as does a father to his sons.

Thus the Son of God—that is to say the word and wisdom of the Father—first found that intellectual faculty of yours which is called reason, fettered by the flesh, a captive to sin, blinded by ignorance, and surrendered to things external. In His mercy He took it up, by His power He raised it, by His wisdom He taught it, drew it to Himself, and in a marvelous manner made it His representative. He then caused it so to sit in judgment upon itself that, with due reverence to the Word with whom it was associated, it might act as its own accuser, witness and judge, and honestly pronounce condemnation on itself. It is from this first alliance between the Word and reason that humility has its origin. We then come to the second faculty, which is called will, and which was contaminated by the poison of the flesh, though this has already been in a measure counteracted by reason. This the Holy Spirit honours with a visit, administers to it a gentle purgative, imparts to it a genial warmth, and thus renders it compassionate; in such a way that after the fashion of a skin which is stretched by the application of an ointment, so the will that has been treated with the heavenly ointment may be so expanded as to become friendly to those that were its enemies. And this second alliance between the spirit of God and the will of man produces love. The Father finally takes the two faculties—reason and will—the one taught by the Word and sprinkled with the hyssop of humility, the other inspired by the spirit of truth and influenced by the fire of love, and unites them into a perfect soul, from which humility has removed all wrinkles and in which love has left no stain. In it will resists not reason. Nor does reason trifle with truth, for the Father unites it to Himself as His glorious bride, in such a way that reason may not be allowed to think of itself, nor will of its neighbour, but the entire delight of that blessed soul will be to say, *The king has taken me into his chamber.* It was fitting, that that soul should first learn in the school of humility under the tuition of the Son, to enter into herself—in accordance with the warning given. *If thou knowest not thyself, go forth and feed thy kids.* (*Cant.* 1:7) Thus did she become fit to be brought from the school of humility under the guidance of the Holy Spirit through affection into the store rooms of love—by which undoubtedly is meant the hearts of her neighbours. Thence, seated on flowers and surrounded by friends, that is, by good habits and holy virtues, she may at last gain entrance to the chamber of the King, for whose love she longs. There, when silence has been made in heaven for a space, it may be of half an hour, she rests calmly in those dear embraces—herself asleep, but her heart on the watch how she may in the present range over those regions of hidden truth—on whose memory she will feast as soon as she returns to herself—there she sees things invisible and hears things unutterable, of which it is not lawful for man to speak. These are the things that surpass all that knowledge which night showeth to night. Yet day unto day throws out language, and the wise are allowed to speak wisdom, and to compare spiritual things with spiritual.

Chapter Eight

The same sequence is seen in the "rapture" of St. Paul to the third heaven.

Do you suppose that St. Paul had not undergone the same gradual process when, as he has told us, he was "caught up" to the third heaven? But why was he "caught up" instead of being "led up"? The reason surely was that if so great an Apostle says that he was "caught up" to a place whither no teaching nor leading could bring him, I, who am certainly a lesser man than Paul, may not venture to think that I can reach the third heaven by any strength or effort of my own; so may I neither trust to strength nor shrink from exertion. For a man who is taught or led is obliged, from the fact that he follows his teacher or leader, to use some effort. He at all events does enough in assisting his removal to the place or condition at which he aims to enable him to say, *Not*

I but the grace of God with me. (*1 Cor.* 15:10). But the man who is carried away, not by his own action, but by that of others, and without even knowing his destination, cannot take the credit or any part of it to himself, since he accomplishes nothing either alone or with assistance. The Apostle might possibly have been directed or assisted to the first or to the middle heaven—to reach the third one he had to be caught up. For the Son is said to have come down for the purpose of helping men to rise to the first, and the Holy Spirit to have been sent to lead them to the second heaven. But the Father, though He always co-operates with the Son and the Holy Spirit, is never said to have come down from heaven, or to have been sent to the earth. It is true that *the earth is full of the mercy of the Lord* (*Ps.* 33:5; 32:5, Vulg.), and that *heaven and earth are full of thy glory*, and much to the same effect. And of the Son I read, *when the fulness of the time came, God sent his Son* (*Gal.* 4:4), and the Son Himself says of Himself, *The Spirit of the Lord hath sent me.* And through the same Prophet He says, *Now the Lord hath sent me and his Spirit.* (*Is.* 38:16). And of the Holy Spirit I read, *The Paraclete, the Holy Ghost, whom the Lord will send in my name* (*John* 14:26), and, *when I have been taken up, I will send him unto you* with undoubted reference to the Holy Spirit. But though there is no region in which the Father does not exist, I find no mention of His own Person anywhere but in heaven, as in the Gospel, my father *who is in heaven* (*Matt.* 16:17), and in the prayer, *Our Father who art in heaven.* (*Matt.* 6:9). From this I unhesitatingly conclude that as the Father did not come down, the Apostle could not go up to the third heaven in order to see Him, though he recalls that he was "caught up" thither. Moreover, *No man hath ascended into heaven, but he that descended from heaven.* (*John* 3:13). And lest you should suppose that the reference here is to the first or second heaven, David tells you, *His going out is from the end of heaven.* (*Ps.* 19:6; 18:7, Vulg.). And to this He was not suddenly caught up, or secretly conveyed, but, as is stated, *in their sight* (*Acts* 1:9) (that is in that of the Apostles) *he was raised up.* It was not with Him, as with Elias who had one witness, or with Paul who could have none, to attest his statement, and who could hardly do so himself, for he admits I know *not, God knoweth.* (*2 Cor.* 12:2). But as the Almighty, He descended and ascended as He pleased, and chose at His discretion, the place, the time, the day and the hour, as well as the onlookers whom He thought worthy to be the witnesses of so great a spectacle, and *while they looked on he was raised up.* Elias and Paul were caught up; Enoch was translated; our Saviour is said to have been taken up, that is to have gone up by Himself, without help from anyone. He depended neither, on conveyance by a chariot, or assistance by an angel, but on His own power. *A cloud received him out of their sight.* (*Acts* 1:9). And what was the purpose of this cloud? Was it to help Him in weakness, to stimulate Him in slackness, or to sustain Him when in danger of falling? Such ideas are inconceivable. That cloud received Him out of the bodily sight of His disciples who, though they had known Him as Christ in the flesh, did not as yet know Him to be more than man. So those whom the Son calls through humility to the first heaven, the Spirit brings together by love in the second, and the Father raises by direct vision to the third. In the first they are humbled by the truth and say, *In thy truth thou hast humbled me.* (*Ps.* 119:75; 118:75, Vulg.). In the second they rejoice together with truth and sing, *Behold how good and how pleasant it is for brethren to dwell together in unity* (*Ps.* 133:1; 132:1, Vulg.)—as also it is written concerning love. *It rejoiceth with the truth.* (*1 Cor.* 13:6). In the third heaven they are carried up to the recesses of truth and say, *My secret to myself, my secret to myself.* (*Is.* 24:16, Vulg. And Sept. and A.V. Marg.)

Chapter Nine

The writer sighs regretfully over his own shortcomings in the search for Truth.

But how can a poor creature like myself ramble on about the two higher heavens in a way more suggestive of the outpouring of words than of spiritual activity, seeing that it is as much as I can do to crawl on my hands and feet under the lower one? Yet I have already, with the help of Him who calls me, set up for myself a ladder to that higher level. I am moving in the direction *wherein I may show to myself the salvation of God.* Now I look upwards to the Lord who is leaning over me, now I spring forward at the call of truth. He has called me and I have answered Him, *to the work of thine hands thou shalt reach out thy right hand.* (*Job* 14:15, Vulg, not A.V.). Thou, Lord, dost indeed number my steps, but I, slow climber and tired traveler, am looking for a resting place by the way. Woe is unto me if the darkness gets hold of me, or if my flight be in the winter or on the sabbath day, yet, though now is the acceptable time, and now is the day of salvation, I delay to set forth towards the light. Why do I thus hold back? Pray for me, son, brother, friend, fellow-traveller with me in the Lord—if such there be. Pray to the Almighty that He will strengthen my feeble foot, yet in such a way that the *foot of pride may not come to me.* (*Ps.* 36:11; 35:12, Vulg.). For though my foot is feeble and unable to attain to the truth, it is more reliable than one which, when it has reached it, cannot stand therein, as you have it in the Psalm, *they are cast out, and could not stand.* (*Ps.* 36:12; 35:13, Vulg.).

So much for the proud. But what about their chief? What about him who is called *king over all the children of pride?* (*Job* 31:25). He, said the Master, *stood not in the truth* (*John* 13:44), and elsewhere, *I saw Satan falling from heaven.* (*Luke* 10:18). Why did he thus fall, unless on account of pride? Woe be to me if he who *knoweth the high afar off* (*Ps.* 137:6), should see me also indulging in pride, and should launch at me the terrible sentence, *Thou wast indeed the son of the most high*, but *as a man thou shalt die, and thou shalt fall like one of the princes.* (*Ps.* 82:6, 7; 81:6, Vulg.). Who would not quail before this voice of thunder? O how much better it was for Jacob that the sinew of his thigh shrank at the touch of the angel than that it should swell, weaken and perish at that of the messenger of pride. Would that an angel would touch my sinew and make it shrink, so that I, who in my own strength cannot but fail, may from my weakness begin to make progress. I surely read, *The weakness of God is stronger than men.* (*1 Cor.* 1:25). So also did the Apostle, when he complained of the sinew which an angel, not of God but of Satan, was buffeting, receive the reply, *My grace is sufficient for thee, for virtue is made perfect in infirmity.* What is this virtue? Let the Apostle himself give the answer, *Gladly therefore will I glory in mine infirmity, that the virtue of Christ may dwell in me.* But you may, perhaps, not quite understand to what virtue he particularly alludes, since Christ possesses all the virtues. But though He has them all, there is one which He pre-eminently possesses and specially commends to us in His own Person, namely, humility, for He says, *Learn of me because I am meek and humble of heart.* (*Matt.* 11:29).

Gladly therefore will I glory in mine infirmity, in the shrinking of my sinew, that thy virtue—which is humility—may be made perfect in me. For thy grace is sufficient for me, when my strength has failed. I will then by thy favour put my foot firmly down, and though through its weakness I must move slowly, I will mount safely by the ladder of humility until, by keeping to the truth, I reach the broad expanse of love. Then will I sing with a gesture of thanks, the words *Thou hast set my feet in a spacious place.* (*Ps.* 31:8; 30:9, Vulg.). Thus by close and careful following of the narrow way, by slow and sure ascent of the steep staircase, with steady but painful progress, I limp along until by some marvelous method, the goal is approached, But *Woe is me* that my *sojourn is prolonged. Who will give me wings like a dove* (*Ps.* 55:6; 54:7, Vulg.), wherewith I may fly more quickly to the truth, and so may rest in love? Since these are wanting, lead me, Lord, in thy way and I will walk in thy truth, and the truth shall set me free. Woe unto me that I ever came down thence. For had I not foolishly and madly begun this descent, I should not have had this long and laborious climb. But why do I speak of a "descent" when I might more accurately call it a "fall"—unless indeed because, as no one comes at once to the top but all have to go up gradually, so no one becomes at once utterly bad but goes gradually downhill. Otherwise how could the saying stand, *The wicked man is proud all the days of his life.* There are, in fact, roads which seem good to men, which yet lead to destruction.

There is then an upward as well as a downward road—a road to good and a road to evil. Avoid the evil and choose the good. If you cannot do this by yourself, pray with the prophet and in his words: *Remove from me the way of iniquity* (*Ps.* 119:29; 118:29, Vulg.), and how shall this be? He adds, *Out of thy law have mercy on me.* This means by the law which thou didst give to those who fainted by the way—that is to those who departed from the truth. And of these I, who have indeed fallen from the truth, am one. But does not a man who has fallen use every effort to rise again? For this reason *I have chosen the way of truth* (*Ps.* 119:30; 118:30, Vulg.), by which I may rise through humility to the place from which I fell through pride. I will rise, say I, and I will sing, *It is good for me, Lord, that thou hast humbled me; the law of thy mouth is good to me, above thousands of gold and silver.* (*Ps.* 119:71, 72; 118:71, 72, Vulg.). David seems to have set before you two roads, which, however, you know to be one—identical yet different—and called by different names—either that of *wickedness* for those who go down, or that of *truth* for those who go up. For you go up to a throne by the same steps by which you come down, you use the same road for approaching or withdrawing from a town, and the same door for entering or leaving a house. In like manner the angels appeared to Jacob as ascending and descending on the same ladder. What do these comparisons suggest? Surely that if you wish to return to the truth, you need not look for a new and unknown road, but for the one by which you know that you came down, so that you may follow your own footsteps, and may humbly rise through the same degrees through which you fell in your pride. That which was the twelfth degree of pride in your fall will be the first degree of humility in your ascent, the eleventh will correspond to the second, the tenth to the third, the ninth to the fourth, the eighth to the fifth, the seventh to the sixth, the sixth to the seventh, the fifth to the eighth, the fourth to the ninth, the third to the tenth, the second to the eleventh and the first to the twelfth. And when you have discovered and really recognized these degrees of pride in yourself, you will have no difficulty in looking for the path of humility.

Part Two

The Twelve Degrees of Pride

Chapter Ten

The first degree—Curiosity.
(The opposite of modesty—especially of the eyes.)

The first degree of pride is curiosity. This you may detect by the following signs. Look at that monk, whom you have hitherto supposed to be a sensible man. He has now taken to staring about him, whether he is standing up, walking about or sitting down. He thrusts his head forward, and pricks up his ears. From his outward movements you can clearly see the inward change that he has undergone. For it is the froward man who *winketh with the eye, presseth with the foot, and speaketh with the finger* (*Prov.* 6:12), and from the unusual movements of his body is seen to have lately contracted disease of the soul—the careless sluggishness of which in self-examination makes it inquisitive about others. So since it takes no heed to itself it is sent out of doors to feed the kids. And as these are the types of sin, I may quite correctly give the title of "kids" to the eyes and the ears, since as death comes into the world through sin, so does sin enter the mind through these apertures. The curious man, therefore, busies himself with feeding them, though he takes no trouble to ascertain the state in which he has left himself. Yet if, O man, you look carefully into yourself, it is indeed a wonder that you can ever look at anything else. You inquisitive fellow, listen to Solomon—you silly fellow, hearken to the wise man, as he says, *With all watchfulness guard thy heart*, in other words, keep all your senses on the watch to protect that which is the source of life. For whither, inquisitive man, will you retire from your own presence—to whom will you in the meantime intrust yourself? How dare you, who have sinned against heaven, lift up your eyes to the sky? Look down to the earth if you want to recognize yourself. It will show you what you are, for *earth thou art, and to earth shalt thou go.* (*Gen.* 3:19, Old Latin).

Now there are two reasons for which you may raise your eyes without being to blame for so doing—one is to seek, the other is to render assistance. David raised his eyes to the mountains for the former, the Lord lifted His over the crowd for the latter purpose. The motive of the one was misfortune; that of the other was mercy, neither was to blame. If you likewise with due regard to place, time and occasion, look up when you or a brother are in distress, I not only do not blame you, I highly commend you. For misfortune allows the one action, mercy approves the other. But in different circumstances I should call you an imitator not of the Prophet nor of the Lord, but of Dina or of Eve, aye, verily, of Satan himself. For Dina when she went out to feed her kids, was snatched away from her father and her maidenhood was taken from her. O Dina, what need was there for thee to look on strange women? Was it necessary—did it serve any useful purpose—or was it done out of mere curiosity? Thy look may have no purpose, but it is not without purpose that men gaze on thee. There is curiosity in thy look, but more in the look that is turned on thee. Who could have supposed that thy curious carelessness or careless curiosity would afterwards prove to be not reckless but ruinous to thee, thy friends and thine enemies?

And thou, O Eve, wast placed in Paradise, that thou mightest work with thine husband and bestow thy care on him; and if thou hadst discharged thy duty, thou wouldst eventually have passed into a better sphere where there would have been no need for thee to be engaged in any work, or to be beset by any care. Leave was given to thee to eat of every tree in Paradise, except that one which is called *the tree of knowledge of good and evil.* (*Gen.* 2:9). For if the others are good and have a good savour, what need is there to eat of one which also has an evil savour? *Not to be more wise than it behoveth to be wise.* For to know evil is not knowledge but folly. So preserve what is given, await what is promised, avoid what is forbidden, lest thou lose what is allowed. Why lookest thou so eagerly for thy death? Why dost thou so often cast in that direction those wandering eyes of thine? What pleasure hast thou in looking on that which thou mayest not eat? Perchance thou dost reply, "I stretch forth mine eyes not my hand. It is not looking but eating that is forbidden. May I not turn those eyes which God has placed under my control in any direction that I please?" To which the Apostle shall answer, *All things are lawful for me, but all things are not expedient.* (*1 Cor.* 6:12). Although it may not be in itself a guilty act, it affords an incentive to sin. For if thy mind had not shown insufficient attention to its own condition, it would have had no time for idle curiosity. Although there may be no offence, there is an opportunity as well as a suggestion to offend and a reason for offending. For while thou art thinking of something else, the serpent creeps craftily into thine heart, and addresses thee in an alluring tone. He overcomes thy reason with his enticements, allays thy fear with falsehoods, and tells thee that thou art in no danger of death. He increases thy distress, as he stimulates thine appetite; he sharpens curiosity and strengthens desire. At length he offers what is forbidden and takes away what is allowed. He presents thee with fruit and deprives thee of Paradise. Thou takest poison: thou wilt perish thyself and wilt bring forth children who will perish. Thou hast sacrificed salvation, without losing the power to give birth. We are born, we die and thus we are born only to die, because we are dead before we are born.

And as for thee, "pattern of perfection," thou wast placed not in Paradise, but in Eden the garden of God. What more couldst thou reasonably desire? Filled with wisdom, and exalted in honour, thou shouldst have expected nothing higher and worked for nothing stronger than thyself. Remain where thou art, lest thou fall from thy position, if thou walkest among things that are too great and wonderful for thee. But why dost thou sometimes turn round and look to the north? I see thee, I already detect thee peering too inquisitively into the unknown heights above thee. *I will place*, sayest thou, my *throne towards the north*. The other dwellers in heaven are standing, whilst thou alone dost desire to sit, and dost thereby disturb the harmony of the brethren, the peace of the whole heavenly community, and, so far as it lies in thy power to do so, the tranquility of the Trinity. Does this curiosity carry thee so far, thou wretched being, that with unrivalled presumption thou dost not scruple to give offence to the citizens and to do injury to the king? *Thousands of thousands minister to him and ten times a hundred thousand stand before him*, where no one is allowed to sit, but He alone who *sitteth upon the cherubims* (*Ps*. 80:1; 79:2, Vulg.) and receiveth the ministrations of others. And dost thou—how shall I put it—claiming a wider outlook, a more incisive scrutiny and a freer entrance than that of the others, place a seat for thyself in heaven, that thou mayest be on a level with the Most High? What is thine object—on what dost thou rely? Thou fool, estimate thy powers, think of the result, consider the process. Dost thou presume on the knowledge or on the ignorance—on the willingness or on the reluctance—of the Most High? But how can He whose purpose is all good, and whose knowledge is unlimited, either consent to or be unaware of, thine evil design? Dost thou think that though He undoubtedly knows and disapproves it, He is unable to prevent it? But unless indeed thou art doubtful whether thou art a created being, I cannot suppose that thou canst doubt the omnipotence, omniscience and excellence of thy Creator, seeing that He was able to create thee out of nothing, and, knowing what thou wouldst turn out to be, willed to make thee the powerful being that thou art. When therefore thou thinkest that God will tolerate that of which He disapproves and has the power to prohibit, do I perchance see in thee the completion—aye, and the origin—of that idea which after thee and because of thee is constantly held by those like thee on earth, and which is embodied in the common saying, "An usurper keeps reckless followers? *Is thine eye evil because he is good?*" (*Matt.* 20:15). This wicked presumption of thine on His benevolence has produced in thee an insolent disregard of His knowledge, and a daring defiance of His power. For this, and nothing less than this, thou unholy one, is thy train of thought. This is the wickedness that thou dost devise on thy bed, and sayest "thinkest thou that the Creator will destroy His own work? I am well aware that no thought of mine escapes God, because He is God, nor does any such thought please Him, because He is good. Nor can I escape His hand—if He so wishes—because He is mighty. But need this be a cause of dread to me? For if through His goodness He can have no pleasure in evil done by me—how much less can He derive it from evil action of His own? I should call it evil on my part to wish to oppose His will—and on His part to avenge Himself. He therefore cannot wish to take vengeance for any crime, since He neither will nor can part with His inherent goodness." It is thyself—thou wretch, alone that thou deceivest, not God. Thou deceivest thyself, I repeat, and thy wickedness lics to thyself not to God. Thou dost indeed act deceitfully, but He detects thy motive. Thus thou deceivest thyself not God. And since in return for His great goodness, thou dost contemplate great evil towards Him, thy wickedness naturally leads thee to hate Him. For what can be more unjust than that the Creator should be scorned by thee for the very reason for which He most deserves thy love? What can be more outrageous than that when thou hast no doubt that the power of God shown in thy creation, could be used for thy destruction, thou dost yet rely on His abundant kindness, and that this should lead thee to hope that He will be unwilling to exercise His vindictive power? Wilt thou repay *good with evil* and *love with hatred?* (*Ps.* 109:5; 108:5, Vulg.).

Now I say that this malice is deserving, not of passing indignation but of abiding wrath. For it is thy desire and hope to be on an equality with the most gracious and most high Lord, although that is not His wish. Thou desirest that He shall have always before His eyes the distressing sight of thine unwelcome presence, and thou thinkest that though He is able to cast thee down, He will not do so, but that He will prefer Himself to suffer than to allow thee to perish. It is undoubtedly in His power to overthrow thee, if such be His will—but in thine opinion His kindness will not allow Him to entertain such a wish. If He be such as thou supposest Him to be, it is clear that thy conduct in not loving Him is so much the baser. And if He does allow action to be taken against Himself rather than take action against thee—how great must be thy malice in having no consideration for Him who disregards Himself in sparing thee? But it is inconceivable that He who is perfect can fail to be both kind and just. It is not as though kindness and justice cannot exist together. Kindness is really better when it is just than when it is slack—nay more, kindness without justice is not a virtue. It therefore appears that thou remainest ungrateful for the loving-kindness of God whereby thou wast created without exertion on thy part, but thou fearest not His justice of which thou hast had no experience, and dost therefore audaciously incur guilt for which thou dost falsely promise thyself impunity. Now mark that thou wilt find Him whom thou hast known to be kind, to be also righteous, and thou wilt thyself fall into the ditch which thou hast dug for thy Creator. Thy design seems to be to inflict on Him an injury which He is able to avoid if He wishes to do so—a wish which thou thinkest that He cannot entertain, as He will not be wanting in that kindness which has led Him never within thine experience to punish anybody. The righteous God will most justly retaliate by punishing thee, since He neither can nor ought to allow such a slight on His goodness to remain unpunished. He may, however, so moderate the severity of His sentence that, if thou art willing to return to reason, He will not refuse thee pardon. But such is *thy hardness and impenitent heart* (*Rom.* 2:5), that thou art incapable of such a wish, and therefore canst not escape the penalty.

But now listen to the accusation against thee. *Heaven*, saith He, *is my throne and the earth my footstool.* (*Is.* 66:1). He did not say "east" or "west," or any one region in the heaven, but the whole heaven is my throne. Thou must not therefore seat thyself in a portion of the heaven, since He has chosen the whole of it for Himself. Thou canst not place thyself on earth, for it is His footstool. For the earth is a solid body, on which is seated the Church, founded on a strong rock. What wilt thou do? Driven out of heaven, thou canst not remain on earth. Choose then for thyself a place in the air, not for session but for flight, so that thou, who didst attempt to shatter the security of eternity, shall pay the penalty of thine own unrest. For, whilst thou art driven to and fro between heaven and earth, the Lord is seated on a *throne high and elevated* (*Is.* 6:1) and the whole earth is full of His majesty—so that thou canst find no place except in the air. For the Seraphim with their wings of contemplation fly from the throne to the footstool, and from the footstool to the throne, while with their other wings they cover the head and feet of the Lord. And I think that they are purposely so placed that, as the access to Paradise was barred against sinful men by the Cherubim, so also shall a limit be set to thy curiosity by the Seraphim. The result will be that thou wilt no longer, with more impudence than prudence, investigate the secrets of heaven, nor wilt thou discover the mysteries of the Church on earth, but shalt find a home only in the hearts of the proud, who neither deign to live on earth like other men, nor fly like the angels to heaven. But although His head is hidden from thee in heaven and His feet on earth, thou mayest as it were be allowed to see—and to envy—some part of what lies between, whilst thou art suspended in the air, and dost behold the angels descending and ascending past thee, though thou art altogether ignorant of what they hear in heaven or tell on earth.

O Lucifer, thou who didst rise in the morning, surely a bearer no longer of light, but of night—aye, even of death—thy proper course was from the east to the south, and dost thou invert the order and perversely tend towards the north? In proportion to thy haste to rise is the rapidity of thy decline and fall. Yet, thou curious one, I should wish to investigate more closely the object of thy curiosity. *I will place*, sayest thou, *my throne towards the north.* And as thou art a spirit, I think that neither "north" nor "throne" is to be understood in a local or literal sense. For I suppose that by "the north" is meant evil men, and by "my throne" thy control over them. For in the foreknowledge of God, thou hast from thy chosen proximity to Him, a clearer insight into the future than had others; and as these were neither enlightened by any ray of wisdom, nor warmed by the love of the spirit, thou didst find in them as it were thine opportunity. Thus didst thou establish thy rule over them, so that thou mightest pour into them some of thy clever cunning, and influence them with thy wicked warmth; so that as the Most High controlled all the sons of obedience by His wisdom and His goodness, thou mightest govern these by thy cunning wickedness and wicked cunning, and in this respect thou mightest resemble Him. But I am surprised that, since in God's foreknowledge thou didst foresee thy rule, thou didst not in like manner foresee thy ruin. For if thou didst foresee it, what madness it was to be so wickedly eager for dominion as to prefer rule and wretchedness to submission and happiness. Or was it not better for thee to be a partner in those regions of light than ruler of those dark places? But it is more likely that thou didst not look forward—either for the reason which I gave above—that in thy reliance on the kindness of God thou didst say in thine heart, *He will not require it* (*Ps.* 10:13), and didst therefore wickedly offend Him, or because when thou didst see thy rule, the beam of pride at once rose up in thine eye—which through its interference was unable to discern its danger.

In like manner Joseph did not foresee his sale though he had foreseen his promotion—and this although the sale was to precede the promotion. I should not from this conclude that the great patriarch was guilty of pride, but that his experience proves that those who possess the spirit of prophecy must not be supposed to have foreseen nothing because they did not foresee everything. Someone may, perhaps, maintain that the fact that this youth recorded his dreams—of whose symbolic significance he was at the time unaware—was a mark of self-sufficiency. I still think that this should be ascribed to their symbolic character or to his boyish innocence, rather than to conceit. And if there were such conceit, he was able to atone for it by his subsequent painful experiences. For revelations of a character pleasing to themselves are sometimes made to certain persons, and though such knowledge must inevitably engender conceit in the human mind, the prediction may nevertheless be fulfilled—albeit in such a way that the vanity which has caused even a slight delight in the importance of the revelation shall not be unpunished. For a physician uses not only ointment but fire and iron, with which he cuts out or cauterizes everything which is useless for the treatment of the wound, so that there may be no obstacle to the remedial working of the ointment. In like manner does God as the physician of souls, prescribe and administer to a soul of such a disposition, temptations and troubles in order that, chastened and humbled, it may turn joy into sorrow, and think the revelation a delusion. The result is that vanity disappears, though the truth of the revelation is not impaired. Thus Paul's tendency to self-exaltation is checked by his thorn in the flesh, while he is himself uplifted by repeated revelations. Thus want of faith in Zacharias is punished by loss of speech, yet the declaration of the angel that the truth would be made clear during his lifetime is unaltered. Thus again, *by honour and dishonor* (*2 Cor.* 6:8) do the saints make progress, though among the special gifts which each receives, they are only too well aware of the existence in them of that vanity which is common to mankind; so that while they know themselves to be the possessors of supernatural favour, they may ever remember whom they truly are.

But what about revelations to mere curiosity? I took the opportunity of dealing with these in a digression, when I tried to show that the wicked angel before his fall was allowed to foresee that dominion which he afterwards acquired over wicked men, but not to anticipate his own condemnation. That is a matter about which questions of small moment may be raised which it is easier to ask than to answer, and of which the sum and substance is but this—that he fell from the truth because his idle speculation led him to unlawful desire and thus to presumptuous aspiration.

Curiosity therefore rightly claims the first place among the degrees of pride, and is thus revealed as the beginning of all sin. But unless this is suppressed very speedily it will soon develop into a careless frame of mind which constitutes the second degree.

Chapter Eleven

The second degree—Levity of mind.
(The opposite of the eleventh degree of humility—
short and sensible speech in a subdued tone.)

For the monk who is careless about himself and unduly inquisitive about other people, looks up to some as his betters and looks down upon others as his inferiors—in some he sees cause for envy, while others are the objects of his scorn. It thus happens that his mind, enervated by his habit of staring about him, is oppressed by no anxiety on its own account, now through pride soars to the heights and then sinks through envy to the depths. He shows at one moment a sulky acquiescence in his own wickedness, at another a childish delight in his excellence. In the former he exhibits his weakness, in the latter his vanity, in both his pride; for it is love of his own excellence that gives him distress when others surpass him, and joy when he surpasses them. This unbalanced disposition shows itself in speech sometimes brief and bitter, sometimes full and feeble, alternately jocose and doleful, and always silly. Compare if you please these two earliest degrees of pride with the two highest degrees of humility, and see if the last one of these latter does not repress curiosity, and the one before it levity. You will find the same contrast if the other degrees are similarly compared. But now let us go on to the study of the third degree—without, however, falling into it.

Chapter Twelve

The third degree—Unseasonable merriment.
(The opposite of the tenth degree of humility—
refraining from frequent and light laughter.)

It is characteristic of the proud that they always look out for pleasure and shun sadness, in accordance with the saying: *The heart of fools is where there is mirth.* (*Eccles.* 7:5; 7:4, A.V.). So it is that the monk who has already descended two degrees of pride and through inquisitiveness has arrived at levity, when he sees the joy for which he is always on the lookout constantly interrupted by the distress which he feels at the sight of good in others, chafes under the sense of humiliation and takes refuge in a suggestion of unreal comfort. Henceforth he restrains his inquisitiveness on that side on which his own worthlessness and his neighbour's excellence are shown to him, and turns his whole attention to the other side. He may thus mark only too carefully those things in which he seems to be the better man, and may hide those in which others surpass him, and so may put away all thought of sorrow and remain always merry. It thus happens that silly merriment soon gains sole possession of the man whom joy and sorrow alternately claim.

I set this before you as the third degree of pride; now note the marks by which you may detect it, either in yourself or in anyone else. You seldom or never hear a man of this kind groan, or see him shed tears. You will think, if you consider, that his faults are either forgotten or forgiven. His gestures are those of a buffoon, his look that of a coxcomb, his step that of a dandy. He is always making jokes, and never loses a chance of laughing. He cuts out of his mind all discreditable and therefore distressing recollections, and concentrates his mental vision on his real or pretended merits. As he thinks of nothing but what is pleasant without considering whether it is lawful, he can neither restrain laughter nor hide his unseasonable merriment. A bladder swells when it is full of wind, but if a small hole is pricked in it and it is squeezed, it creaks as it collapses, and the air does not rush out at once, but is gradually expelled and gives out frequent intermittent sounds. In like manner when a monk has filled his mind with vapid and vulgar thoughts, the flood of folly which cannot, owing to the rule of silence, find full and free vent, is thrown out from his narrow jaws in guffaws of laughter. He constantly hides his face as if ashamed, compresses his lips, and clenches his teeth. He laughs loudly without meaning to do so, and even against his will. And when he has stopped his mouth with his fists he is frequently heard to sneeze.

Chapter Thirteen

The fourth degree—Boastfulness.
(The opposite of the ninth degree of humility, reticence until questioned.)

But when vanity increases, and the bladder begins to be inflated, it becomes necessary to loosen the belt and allow a larger outlet for the air, otherwise the bladder will burst. So the monk who is unable to discharge his superabundant store of unseemly merriment by laughter or by gesture, breaks forth with the words of Elihu, *My belly is as new wine which wanteth vent, which bursteth the new vessels.* (*Job* 32:19). He must speak out or break down. *For he is full of matter to speak of, and the spirit of his bowels constraineth him.* (*Ibid.*, 5:18). He hungers and thirsts for hearers, at whom he may throw his banalities, to whom he may pour out his feelings, and let them know what a fine fellow he is. But when he has found his opportunity of speaking—if the conversation turns on literary matters, old and new points are brought forward; he airs his ideas in loud and lofty tone. He interrupts his questioner and answers before he is asked. He himself puts the question and gives the answer, nor does he even allow the person to whom he is talking to finish his remarks. When the striking of the silence gong puts a stop to conversation, he complains that a full hour is not a sufficient allowance, and asks for indulgence that he may go on with his gossip after the time for it is over—not to add to the knowledge of any one else, but to boast of his own. He has the power but not the purpose of giving useful information. His care is not to teach you or to learn from you things which he does not know, but that the extent of his learning may be made known. If the subject under discussion is religion, he is forward with his vision and his dreams. He upholds fasting, prescribes vigils, and maintains the paramount importance of prayer. He enlarges at great length but with excessive conceit on patience, humility and all the virtues in turn, with the intention that you on hearing him should say, *Out of the abundance of the heart the mouth speaketh* (*Matt.* 12:34, 35), *and that a good man out of his good treasure bringing forth good things.* If the talk turns on light subjects he becomes more loquacious, because he is on more familiar ground. If you hear the torrent of his conceit you may say that his mouth is a fount of such buffoonery as to move even strict and sober monks to light laughter. To put it shortly, mark his swagger in his chatter. In this you have the name and description of the fourth degree of pride. Remember the description and avoid the reality. With this warning, go on to the fifth degree which I call eccentricity.

Chapter Fourteen

The fifth degree—Eccentricity.
(The opposite of the eighth degree of humility, observance of the general rule of the monastery.)

A man who prides himself on being better than his fellow-men thinks it a disgrace if he does not do something more than they do, whereby his superiority may be apparent. Therefore the general rule of the monastery and the example of its senior members are not enough for him. Yet his anxiety is not to be, but to be seen to be better than they. His effort is not to lead a better life but visibly to surpass others, so that he may be able to say, *I am not as the rest of men.* (*Luke* 18:11). He takes more credit to himself for having once gone without a meal while others were having theirs, than he does in having shared in a fast of seven days. One little private prayer of his own seems to him more commendable than the recitation of all the Psalms set for an entire night. At mealtime he has a habit of casting his eyes all round the tables, and if he sees anyone eating less than himself, he is annoyed at being outdone. He begins severely to cut down the amount of food which he had hitherto recognized as his necessary ration, because he is more afraid of loss of credit than of the pangs of hunger. If he catches sight of anyone more shrunken and sallow than himself, he cannot rest under what he considers to be a disgrace. And, since he cannot see his own face and the aspect under which he presents himself to onlookers, he examines his hands and arms which he can see, beats his breast, taps his shoulders and loins, and from the more or less attenuated condition of his limbs forms an opinion as to the paleness or colour of his face. But while active in all his private devotions, he is indolent in public worship. He keeps vigil while in bed, and goes to sleep in his stall. He sleeps all night while others are chanting the early Psalms. When the vigil is over, and the other monks are resting in the cloister, he alone lingers in the oratory. He coughs and spits, and the ears of those sitting outside are filled with the sighs and groans from his corner. By his silly and singular action he has established a high reputation with his more simple brethren, who quite approve what they see of his doings, though they do not detect their motive, and, by the commendation which they bestow on him, they aid and abet the wretched man's mistake.

Chapter Fifteen

Sixth degree—Conceit.
(The opposite of the seventh degree of humility—belief and acknowledgment of one's inferiority to others.)

He believes what he hears, praises his own action, and pays no attention to the motive. He welcomes a favourable opinion and forgets its purpose. And he who in everything else puts more trust in himself than in other men, attaches more weight to the opinions of others about him than to his own. So not only does he think that he exhibits superior religion on account of his verbal profession or special display of piety, but in his inmost heart he considers himself more holy than anyone else. And if he knows that he is praised for anything, he ascribes it, not to the ignorance or the kindliness of the person who commends him, but, with much conceit, to his own deserts. So after eccentricity, conceit has made good its claim to be the sixth degree. After it, audacity shows itself—and in it the seventh degree consists.

Chapter Sixteen

Seventh degree—Audacity.
(The opposite of the sixth degree of humility—
acknowledgment of oneself as unworthy and useless.)

For if a man thinks himself superior to others, is it likely that he will not push himself in front of them? He is the first to take his seat at meetings, the first to intervene in debate. He comes forward without invitation, and with no introduction but his own; he re-opens questions that have been settled, and goes again over work that has been done. He considers that nothing that he has not himself designed and carried out, has been properly organized or satisfactorily executed. He criticizes those who sit in judgment, and tells them what their decisions should be. If, when the time comes for the appointment of a Prior, he is not promoted to the office, he is certain that his Abbot is either jealous or mistaken.

But if some less important duty is assigned to him, he is displeased and contemptuous, for, as he feels himself qualified for greater work, he thinks that he ought not to be employed in smaller matters. But it is inconceivable that a man who, with more rashness than readiness, is very anxious to undertake all sorts of work, should not sometimes make mistakes. And it is the duty of the Abbot to reprove such an one for his error. But how will he confess his fault, if he neither thinks himself, nor will allow others to think him, worthy of censure? Therefore when his fault is pointed out to him, it is not removed but grows worse. So if, when he is reproved, you see him incline his heart to wicked words, you may know that he has sunk to the eighth degree, which is called defense of wrong-doing.

Chapter Seventeen

The eighth degree—Defense of wrong-doing.
(The opposite of the fifth degree of humility—a humble and straightforward disclosure of sins and evil thoughts.)

There are many ways in which defense is made for sin. A man either says "I did it not" or "I no doubt did it, but I acted rightly in so doing," or "I may have acted wrongly but not to a serious extent," or, "If I was seriously wrong, I had no bad intention." If, however, he, like Adam and Eve, is proved to be guilty, he attempts to excuse himself on the ground that he was tempted by someone else. But if a man unblushingly defends even open sins, will he ever humbly disclose to the Abbot the hidden evil thoughts which come into his mind?

Chapter Eighteen

The ninth degree—Dishonest confession.
(The opposite of the fourth degree of humility, willing endurance of hardship as a matter of obedience.)

But although defenses of this kind are considered so wrong that they are called by the Prophet *evil words* (*Ps*. 141:4; 140:4, Vulg.), a false and perverse confession is much more dangerous than ever a brazen and stubborn defense. For there are some who, when they are reproved for rather conspicuous offences, and know that no excuse which they may offer will be accepted, have recourse to a more cunning form of defense—they reply by a deceitful confession. *For there is*, as it is written, *one that humbleth himself wickedly and his interior is full of deceit.* The countenance is downcast—the body is prostrate. They exact from themselves, if they are able to do so, some tears. They interrupt their speech by sighs and intersperse their words with groans. A man of this description not only offers no excuse for the offences with which he is charged, but himself even exaggerates his guilt. He does this that you, when you hear him make a further accusation against himself of some impossible or inconceivable crime, may be disposed to disbelieve even that of which you thought him guilty—and thus, from the fact that he makes a confession which you fully believe to be false, some doubt may be thrown on that which you held to be almost certain. And when these men make a statement the acceptance of which they do not desire, by their confession they excuse, and by their disclosures they conceal, their fault. Their confession sounds praiseworthy in the mouth, but wickedness is hidden in the heart; so that he who hears may think that the confession is made with more humility than accuracy, and may apply to them that Scriptural saying, *The righteous man at the beginning of his speech is his own accuser.* For in the sight of men they would rather be thought wanting in truthfulness than in humility—while in the sight of God they are lacking in both. But if their guilt is so clear that by no subterfuge can it be entirely concealed, they nevertheless adopt the tone, though not the spirit of repentance, and by this means remove the mark, though not the reality of their guilt, as they make up for ignoring an open offence by the credit of a public confession.

A fine sort of humility is this, in which pride seeks to array itself, that it may not lose caste! But this double-dealing is soon detected by the Abbot, unless he is to some extent imposed upon by this haughty humility, and thus induced to pass over the fault or postpone the penalty. *The furnace trieth the potter's vessels* (*Ecclus.* 27:6), and distress reveals the real penitent. For the man who is truly penitent does not shrink from the trouble of repentance. Whatever is prescribed to him on account of the fault which he detests, he accepts with submissive and silent acquiescence. And if through this very obedience unexpected hardships arise, and he thereby sustains injuries that were not intended, he does not give up, so that he may show that he has his place in the fourth degree of humility. But he whose confession is unreal, when he is confronted with a slight rebuke, or trifling penalty, is unable either to feign humility or to conceal his dissimulation. He murmurs, gnashes his teeth and loses his temper, and it becomes clear that, so far from standing in the fourth degree of humility, he has fallen into the ninth degree of pride, which from the above description of it, may well be called sham confession. How great, think you, must be the proud man's consternation when his deceit is detected, his pardon forfeited, and his fault not condoned? He is at last found out and condemned by all—and the general indignation is all the greater when men see how erroneous was their former judgment of him. It is then the duty of the Abbot to be less ready to pardon him, because the forgiveness of one would be an offence to all.

Chapter Nineteen

The tenth degree—Rebellion.
(The opposite of the third degree of humility—
obedient submission to superiors.)

Unless by a merciful intervention of Providence this man quietly accepts the unanimous verdict—a thing which it is very difficult for such persons to do—he soon becomes shameless and defiant, and more hopelessly degenerate, and sinks through rebellion into the tenth degree, so that he who had hitherto by his conceit treated his brethren with veiled discourtesy, now by his disobedience shows open contempt for authority. For it should be observed that all the degrees—which I have divided into twelve—may be arranged in three groups; in the first six there is disrespect to the brethren, in the four that follow defiance of authority, while the last two show complete contempt for God. And it should also be noted that, just as the first two degrees in the ascending scale of humility must be attained before entering the community so the last downward steps in pride, which are their counterpart, cannot be taken whilst in it. That the first two degrees must be previously passed, the language of the Rule makes clear. For it says that "The third degree is that anyone for love of God should submit with entire obedience to his superior." (*Rule*, cap. 7). Therefore if this submission, which beyond doubt is made when the novice enters the convent, is assigned to the third degree, the necessary presumption is that the two preceding degrees have been passed. Therefore when a monk scorns alike the harmony of the brethren and the decision of his ruler, what more can he do in the monastery except cause scandal?

Chapter Twenty

Eleventh degree—Freedom to sin.
(The opposite of the second degree of humility—
forbearance to press personal desire.)

So after the tenth degree—which has been described as "rebellion"—the man is at once caught in the eleventh. He then enters those paths which are attractive to men, at the end of which (unless God shall perchance have interposed some barrier for his protection) he will be plunged into the nethermost hell—that is into contempt of God.

For *the wicked man when he is come into the depth of evils, contemneth.* (*Prov.* 28:3, Old Latin). The eleventh degree may be called freedom to sin, since in it a monk, who sees that he has now neither a ruler to fear nor brethren to respect, can safely and freely give full play to his own desires, which shame as well as fear prevented him from doing while in the monastery. But although he no longer dreads his brethren or his Abbot, he has not yet lost all awe of God. Reason, some faint echo of which still remains, places this check upon his inclination, and it is not without some hesitation that he enters on his sinful course, and, like a man who is trying to ford a stream, steps rather than runs into the torrent of vice.

Chapter Twenty-One

Twelfth degree—Habitual sin.
(The opposite of the first degree of humility—constant abstinence from sin for fear of God.)

But when, by the awful judgment of God, his first offences have been unpunished, the pleasure that he has derived from them is freely repeated, and its repetition engrosses him. Lust is quickened, reason lulled, and habit becomes bondage. The wretched man is drawn into the abyss of evil, made prisoner to the despotic rule of vice, and so overwhelmed by the whirlpool of his carnal desires that he forgets alike his own reason and the fear of God, and says madly in his heart, *There is no God*, He now, without scruple, puts pleasure in the place of law, his mind, his hands and his feet are no longer forbidden to consider, execute and pursue courses that are unlawful; but whatever comes to his heart, his mouth or his hand, he designs, discusses and carries out, with evil intent, idle utterance, and sinful action. Just as a righteous man, when he has risen through all the degrees, is able by his habitual goodness to run eagerly and easily to life; so does the wicked man, who has gone down through the same degrees, in consequence of his evil practice emancipated from the rule of reason and unrestrained by the bridle of fear, hasten undaunted to his death. There are some in the middle who are wearied and worried—who, alternately tortured by the fear of hell, and hindered by longstanding habit, find the descent or ascent hard work. The first one and the last one alone move quickly and without hindrance. The latter hastens to death—the former to life—the one more speedily, the other with greater care. Love makes the one eager, lust renders the other inert. The affection of the one, the indifference of the other make both insensible to toil. So in the one perfect love, in the other consummate wickedness drives out fear. Loyalty gives confidence to the one; blindness does the same for the other. So the twelfth degree may be called the habit of sinning, because in it the fear of God is lost, and its place is taken by scorn.

Chapter Twenty-Two

To what extent may prayer be offered for the incorrigible, and spiritually dead?

For *such an one*, says John the Apostle, *I do not say that any one shall pray.* But sayest thou, O Apostle, that no one may hope? Surely he who loves that man may groan. He ventures not to pray, he need not forbear to weep. What is this that I say—that perchance there remains the resource of hope, where prayer has no place? Take an instance of one who believes and hopes, yet does not pray. *Lord*, she says, *if thou hadst been here, my brother had not died.* (*John* 11:21). What mighty faith to believe that by His presence the Lord could have prevented death. But what comes next? It is inconceivable that she should doubt that He whom she believed could have kept him alive, was unable to raise him from the dead. *But now*, says she, *I know that whatsoever thou wilt ask of God, God will give it thee.* (*John* 11:22). Then when He asks where they had laid him, she replies, *Come and see.* (*John* 11:34). Why dost thou stop there? O Martha, thou dost afford to us ample evidence of thy faith; but, as it is so great, why dost thou hesitate? *Come*, sayest thou, *and see.* Why, if thou art not without hope, dost not thou go further and say, "and raise him up"? If, on the other hand, thou art in despair, why givest thou the Master unreasonable trouble? Is it perchance that faith sometimes obtains that for which we dare not pray? Then as He approaches the corpse thou dost object to His coming near, and sayest, *Lord, by this time he stinketh, for he hath been dead four days.* Was this said in despair, or in pretence? In somewhat the same sense the Lord Himself after His Resurrection *made as though he would go further* (*Luke* 24:28), while His intention was to remain with the disciples. O ye holy women, intimate friends of Christ, if ye love your brother why do ye not appeal to the compassion of Him of whose power and pity ye cannot entertain a doubt? Their answer is, "We pray all the better for not uttering a prayer, we trust the more completely for concealing our confidence. We show our faith and suppress our feelings. He who has no need of any information Himself knows what we desire. We indeed know that He can do all things; but a miracle so great, so unprecedented, though it is within

His power, far surpasses anything that in our insignificance we deserve. It is enough for us to have afforded scope for his power and an opportunity for His pity and we prefer patiently to await His will than daringly to demand that which it may not be His pleasure to give. And finally our modesty may perhaps obtain for us something more than we deserve."

And I observe that Peter wept after his serious fall, but I do not hear that he prayed. Yet I have no doubt about his pardon.

Learn further from the Mother of the Lord how to have full faith in the marvelous and in the fullness of faith to preserve modesty. Learn to adorn faith with modesty and to avoid presumption. *They have no wine* (*John* 2:3), says she. With what brevity, with what reverence she made a suggestion on a matter in which she felt a kindly anxiety. And that you may learn in similar circumstances rather to heave a sympathetic sigh than to venture to make a direct request, she concealed her eager earnestness under a shade of shyness, and modestly refrained from expressing the confidence she felt in prayer. She did not come boldly forward with a clear request, and say straight out before every one "I appeal to thee, my son: the wine has run short, the guests are annoyed, the bridegroom is dismayed—show what thou canst do." But although as her breast was burning with these and many other thoughts, she might have expressed her feelings warmly, yet the devout Mother quietly approached her mighty Son, not to test His power but to discover His will. *They have no wine*, says she. How could she better have combined modesty and confidence? There was no lack of faith in her devotedness, of seriousness in her voice, or of earnestness in her desire. She, however, though she was His Mother, waived the claims of kinship, and did not venture to ask for a miraculous supply of wine. With what face, then, can I, a common slave, to whom it is a high honour to be in the service at once of the Son and of the Mother, presume to ask for the life of one who has been dead for four days?

It is also recorded in the Gospel that two blind men had sight given or restored to them—one the sight which he had lost, the other that which he had never possessed—for one had become blind, the other had been so born. But the one who had lost his sight earned marvelous mercy by piteous and persistent prayer, while the one who was born blind received from his divine enlightener a yet more merciful and more marvelous benefit without any previous petition from himself. To him it was afterwards said, *Thy faith hath made thee whole.* (*Luke* 28:42). I also read of the raising of two persons who had lately died—

and of a third one who had been dead for four days; but only the one who was still lying in her father's house was thus raised at his prayer—the other two were restored by a great and unexpected manifestation of mercy.

So if, in like manner, it should happen (which may God avert) that any one of our brethren should meet not bodily but spiritual death; as long as he shall be with us, I, sinner that I am, will persistently assail the Saviour with my prayers and with those of the brethren. If he revives, we shall have gained our brother; but if we do not deserve to be heeded and the time comes when he cannot endure those who are alive, or be endured by them, but must be carried out for burial, I go on faithfully with my mourning, though I cannot pray with so much confidence. I dare not say openly, "Lord raise up our dead brother," but with anxious heart and inward trembling I cease not to cry out. If by any chance at all the Lord shall listen to the desire of the poor, his ear will heed the readiness of their hearts. And there is that saying, *Wilt thou show wonders to the dead? or shall physicians raise to life and give praise to thee?* (*Ps.* 88:10; 878:11, Vulg.) and concerning him who has been dead four days. *Shall anyone in the sepulcher declarethy mercy; and thy truth in destruction?* (*Ps.* 88:10; 87:12, Vulg.). Meanwhile it is possible that the Saviour may be pleased to meet us unforeseen and unexpectedly, and moved by the tears, not by the prayers of the bearers, to restore the dead man to those who live, or actually to recall from among the dead one who is already buried. But I should describe as dead the man who by excusing his sins, has already come down to the eighth degree. For *praise perisheth from the dead as from one who does not exist.* But after the tenth degree, which is third from the eighth, he is already being carried out into liberty to sin, when he is expelled from the monastic community. But after he has passed the fourth degree he is rightly said to be "four days dead," and when he falls into the fifth degree of habitual sin he is already buried. But God forbid that we should cease to pray in our hearts for such even as these—though we do not venture to do so openly, as Paul also mourned for those whom he knew to have died impenitent. For although they shut themselves out from our united prayers, they cannot altogether do so from their effects. They should nevertheless realize the great danger which those incur whom the Church, which prays confidently for Jews, heretics and heathen, dares not to mention in her worship. For when on Good Friday prayer is expressly offered for certain wicked persons, no mention is made of those who are excommunicated.

You may perhaps say, brother Godfrey, that in thus describing the degrees of pride instead of those of humility,

I seem to have gone beyond your request and my own tardy promise. To which my answer is that I was unable to teach anything but what I had learned. I did not think it seemly on my part to speak of an ascent, since I am aware that my own movements have been in a downward rather than in an upward direction. Blessed Benedict may set before you the degrees of humility, for he has previously set his own heart upon them. I have nothing to put before you, unless it be my own downward course. Yet if that is carefully examined, the way to go up may haply be found therein. For if as you are going towards Rome, a man who is coming thence meets you, and you ask him the way, how can he better tell you than by pointing out the route that he has followed? In naming the castles, villages, cities, rivers and mountains which he has passed, he records his own journey and foretells yours, so that as you go on you may recognize the places that he has passed. In like manner in this downward course of mine you may possibly discover the upward steps, and as you ascend, may you study them to more purpose in your own heart than in my book.